SUPPORTING

DIFFERENTIATED INSTRUCTION

A Professional Learning Communities Approach

ROBIN J. FOGARTY / BRIAN M. PETE

FOREWORD BY Jay McTighe

Solution Tree | Press

555 North Morton Street
Bloomington, IN 47404

800.733.6786 (toll free) / 812.336.7700
FAX: 812.336.7790

email: info@solution-tree.com
solution-tree.com

Visit **go.solution-tree.com/instruction** to download the reproducibles in this book.

Printed in the United States of America

19 18   4 5

Library of Congress Cataloging-in-Publication Data

Fogarty, Robin.

   Supporting differentiated instruction : a professional learning communities approach / Robin J. Fogarty, Brian M. Pete.

      p. cm.

   Includes bibliographical references and index.

   ISBN 978-1-935249-55-9 (perfect-bound) -- ISBN 978-1-935249-56-6 (library binding) 1. Individualized instruction--United States. 2. Inclusive education--United States. 3. Mainstreaming in education--United States. 4. Classroom management--United States. I. Pete, Brian M. II. Title.

   LC1201.M37 2010

   371.39'4--dc22

                              2010026861

Solution Tree
Jeffrey C. Jones, CEO & President

Solution Tree Press
President: Douglas M. Rife
Publisher: Robert D. Clouse
Vice President of Production: Gretchen Knapp
Managing Production Editor: Caroline Wise
Copy Editor: Rachel Rosolina
Proofreader: Sarah Payne-Mills
Cover and Text Designer: Orlando Angel

To Brian's sister, Barbara Frances Santoro,
for her thirty years of dedicated work with
intellectually challenged young adults

ACKNOWLEDGMENTS

Our gratitude goes to Howard Gardner and Carol Ann Tomlinson for their pioneering work. Their theories have changed the worldview of the human mind and its propensities for learning.

Our appreciation goes to Shirley Hord, Rick and Becky DuFour, Robert Eaker, and Mike Schmoker for their groundbreaking work. They have released teachers from behind closed doors to the collaborative community of professional learners.

Our acknowledgment goes to the reviewers, editors, proofreaders, and production staff for their painstaking work. They have managed their publishing roles and deadlines with precision and panache.

Solution Tree Press would like to thank the following reviewers:

Barbara Arnold
Leadership Development Consultant
Ottawa Catholic School Board
Ottawa, Ontario

Dixon Brooks
Principal
Fulmer Middle School
West Columbia, South Carolina

Paul Farmer
Professional Learning Communities at
  Work™ Associate
Solution Tree
Fairfax, Virginia

Robin Hartman
Seventh-Grade Language Arts and
  Reading Teacher
Bear Valley Middle School
Escondido, California

Debra McClanahan
Director of Professional Development
Marana Unified School District
Marana, Arizona

Deborah McDonough
Second-Grade Teacher
Roosevelt Elementary
Tampa, Florida

TABLE OF CONTENTS

Visit **go.solution-tree.com/instruction** to download the reproducibles in this book.

Italicized entries indicate reproducible pages.

ABOUT THE AUTHORS

 **Robin J. Fogarty**, PhD, is president of Robin Fogarty & Associates, a Chicago-based, minority-owned educational publishing and consulting company. Her doctorate is in curriculum and human resource development from Loyola University of Chicago. A leading proponent of the thoughtful classroom, Robin has trained educators throughout the world in curriculum, instruction, and assessment strategies. She has taught at all levels, from kindergarten to college, served as an administrator, and consulted with state departments and ministries of education in the United States, Puerto Rico, Russia, Canada, Australia, New Zealand, Germany, Great Britain, Singapore, Korea, and the Netherlands. Robin has published articles in *Educational Leadership*, *Phi Delta Kappan*, and the *Journal of Staff Development*. She is the author of numerous publications, including *Brain-Compatible Classrooms*, *Ten Things New Teachers Need*, *Literacy Matters*, *How to Integrate the Curricula*, *Close the Achievement Gap*, *Informative Assessment: When It's Not About a Grade*, *Twelve Brain Principles That Make the Difference*, and *Nine Best Practices That Make the Difference*. Her recent work includes the two-book leadership series, *From Staff Room to Classroom*.

Brian M. Pete is cofounder of Robin Fogarty & Associates, an educational consulting and publishing company. He comes from a family of educators—college professors, school superintendents, teachers, and teachers of teachers. He has a rich background in professional development. Brian has worked and taped classroom teachers and professional experts in schools throughout the United States, Europe, Asia, Australia, and New Zealand. He has an eye for the "teachable moment" and the words to describe what he sees as skillful teaching. Brian's educational videos include *Best Practices: Classroom Management* and *Best Practices: Active Learning Classrooms.* He is coauthor of ten books, which include *Data Driven Decisions, Twelve Brain Principles That Make the Difference, Nine Best Practices That Make the Difference, The Adult Learner,* and *A Look at Transfer.* His most recent publications, *From Staff Room to Classroom I* and *II,* target change agents in schools.

FOREWORD

JAY McTIGHE

The words of the classic Bob Dylan song "The Times They Are A-Changin'" could not more accurately describe aspects of education today. In particular, the professional demands of teaching have undergone striking shifts in recent years, and this book reflects two of the most noteworthy.

Permit a bit of nostalgia here. I began teaching in 1971 during a very different era. Not only were we teachers neither obligated to uphold academic standards, nor held accountable for the results of high-stakes testing, but administrative expectations were much more lenient. For instance, in my school, virtually any teacher would be rated as "satisfactory" who received few parental complaints and who addressed behavior problems primarily in the classroom instead of bumping them to the front office. In those days, much less attention was paid to learning results, in part because appropriate measures were lacking. Achievement tests, such as the Iowa Test of Basic Skills, were norm referenced, not standards based, and their results were often cited to justify educators' perceptions of student aptitudes. Moreover, it was widely assumed that learners' intellectual capabilities were largely fixed at birth, could be quantified as an intelligence quotient (IQ) score, and were spread across a bell-shaped curve. This seemed fine, since prevailing one-size-fits-all methods of teaching were likely to yield just such an achievement curve, thus reinforcing the expectations that some learners had "it" and some didn't. The consequences of failure to fully develop the talents of all students were not so dire, since in those days there were still many well-paying jobs in the trades and factories that did not require a higher education. In fact, I remember a prevailing norm in my school: "higher-order skills for the gifted, basic skills for the rest."

Fast-forward forty years. My youngest daughter is now studying to be a teacher, and she will enter a profession with very different opportunities, challenges, and expectations. Not only will she serve an increasingly diverse population of learners, she will be expected to move *all* students toward rigorous academic standards and 21st century skills. She will encounter an educational system that has shifted from focusing on inputs and process to one that emphasizes results. Additionally, the guiding beliefs about learning have a-changed. Intelligence is no longer conceived as a single, fixed entity. Neuroscientists have documented the extraordinary plasticity of the brain to change and grow in dramatic ways, and learners are believed to have varying degrees of strengths in *multiple* intelligences. The emergence of powerful information technologies and a global economy have "flattened" the world. Not only have many manufacturing jobs moved offshore to lower-wage workplaces, but increasingly high-skilled occupations are similarly relocating. A world-class education is imperative for individuals and nations.

Such seismic shifts, within and beyond the education establishment, beckon us to consider the two ideas conjoined in this book—differentiated instruction and professional learning communities. Differentiated instruction logically extends from a straightforward proposition—that learners differ in their prior knowledge and experience, their interests, and their preferred ways of learning. Accordingly, the most effective teaching responds to these differences by adjusting (differentiating) how content is presented, how learners are able to process it, and how they are allowed to demonstrate their learning. We now recognize that a one-size-fits-all instructional approach is unlikely to maximize achievement for all learners. Indeed, the goal of helping all students achieve high standards *demands* instruction that is responsive to their varied nature and needs.

The emergence of the PLC movement in recent years reflects yet another paradigm shift in the profession. Back in my day, teachers' work was a largely solitary and private experience, divorced from other adults in the school building. While I enjoyed the company of (most of) my fellow teachers, professional collaboration was not the norm. Indeed, the unstated rule was that teachers went into their rooms, closed the doors, did their thing, and didn't let anyone get too close. It was decidedly *not* the norm to share lessons or unit plans, let anyone watch your teaching (other than the obligatory and often perfunctory administrative observation), nor examine learning results or student work in teams. When students were falling behind academically, it was assumed that they were simply reflecting the lower side of the expected curve. In cases of more severe achievement deficits, they were referred to special education and pulled out of regular classes.

Today, the game has changed. Teachers increasingly operate as members of PLCs within and across grades and subject areas. PLC members typically engage as teams to map the curriculum and design units, analyze achievement data from external test results, and examine student work derived from common assessments. Student learning results lead to collaboratively developed plans to address areas of need, and teachers plan a pyramid of interventions, sharing their best ideas and resources for both remediation and enrichment.

While the topics of differentiated instruction and PLCs are typically addressed independently, authors Robin Fogarty and Brian Pete weave the two into a seamless garment. The book proposes a pathway toward true *professional* development that honors the professionalism of teachers while concurrently targeting the achievement needs of the academically diverse learners they serve.

While each major chapter includes summaries of relevant theories and research, the book is anything but "ivory tower" in its orientation. Instead, the emphasis is pragmatic. The authors marry analytic insight with the practical wisdom of veteran educators as they share a variety of proven techniques for building teams, forging shared beliefs, dissecting data, attaining consensus, and teaching responsively.

This book is kaleidoscopic in that it offers many individual gems that combine to form powerful mosaics for teaching, learning, and professional collaboration. As a beginning teacher, my daughter will benefit from reading it. You will as well.

INTRODUCTION

PLCS AND DIFFERENTIATED INSTRUCTION

PLC TAKE AWAY

Learning How Collaboration Supports Substantive Change

Supporting Differentiated Instruction: A Professional Learning Communities Approach strives for a pragmatic approach to both the collaborative spirit of professional learning communities (PLCs) and the rigorous work of differentiated classroom instruction. One is about teaching decisions for professional staff, the other about learning decisions for students. As the discussion unfolds, we examine this teaching-learning equation in the practical light of how PLCs provide the decision-making platform for differentiated classroom instruction.

As team members soon find out, there is more to a PLC than simply coming together. The meeting times have been scheduled, the PLC notebooks are out, and the teacher teams are in place; everything is where it should be, but what is the next step? The teachers know what they want to happen, but aren't sure how to move the scenario along on their own.

Differentiated learning in the classroom can cause a comparable dilemma. A social studies teacher knows exactly how to follow the basic lesson—how to plan the instruction, introduce the vocabulary, integrate relevant activities, and create key assignments, and when to ask the essential questions to begin student projects. She knows that this will suit the majority of her social studies students, who have come to expect and even favor her style and order of teaching. However, she doesn't always know how to differentiate this standard lesson for those who are struggling, need motivation, or require more challenging choices.

There is need for further understanding, information, and collaboration to support differentiation within a PLC approach. While all classroom teachers differentiate instruction in some fundamental way, the challenge is in developing reflective teachers who can identify *what* to differentiate, *how* to differentiate it, and explain *why* they differentiate it. A PLC provides the structure for those all-important collegial conversations that support foundational questions and critical decisions about differentiating classroom instruction.

Teachers need plausible methods to put these profound theories of collaboration and differentiation into classroom practice. In short, teachers need a framework to guide them in fostering differentiated instruction from the PLC to the K–12 classroom; *Supporting Differentiated Instruction: A Professional Learning Community Approach* is that guide.

Supporting Differentiated Instruction provides teachers with the tools and techniques for reflective dialogue. More specifically, the discussion offers ideas to support meaningful decisions with plain talk about accessible, ongoing data and the instructional tools needed for robust differentiation in classroom instruction. A PLC approach to differentiated instruction trusts the teachers and the learners. It differs and it differentiates. It converses and it collaborates. It meanders and it measures. And in the end, it instructs and inspires by consistently and continually putting kids first.

About the Book

> **PLC TAKE AWAY**
>
> Learning How PLCs Use This Resource to Promote Student Success

Supporting Differentiated Instruction is arranged around a teaching-and-learning discussion focused on supporting differentiating instruction with a PLC approach. Some PLCs, teams within PLCs, or single readers may want to proceed chronologically, moving from chapter to chapter. They might choose to create an extended book study or use the chapters as a roadmap. Others may choose to dip in and out of the chapters, targeting particular elements that match their own progress in the differentiation process.

The chapters can either stand alone or create a comprehensive view of differentiated instruction through a PLC approach. Each chapter begins with a Take Away objective that guides the discussion and ends with Action Options of highly interactive strategies based on the chapter's Take Away. We've designed these tools for teams to utilize as they unpack the complex process of sustaining and facilitating differentiated instruction. At the end of the day, the goal is to help PLC teams manage the complexity of the instructional arena in ways that personalize instruction for the success of each and every student in the system.

Following are chapter summaries designed to help you decide how best to approach this resource.

Chapter 1: All About Collaboration

Chapter 1 is framed by the Take Away "Learning How PLCs Support Student Success." This first chapter addresses the most fundamental logistics of working within the culture of professional learning communities. It also outlines the many decisions necessary for PLCs to function fully and effectively by discussing the key questions of who, what, when, where, why, and how.

Chapter 2: All About Differentiation

Chapter 2 develops the complex concept of differentiated instruction. The Take Away targets the essence of that discussion: "Learning How Differentiation Addresses Student Needs." We explain both an explicit and an implicit model of defining differentiation in this chapter. The goal, of course, is to present a viable understanding for all stakeholders in PLC teams as teachers pursue the process of developing and designing a more differentiated approach to instruction. The important message in this chapter is that PLC team members need to come to an agreement and develop a working consensus on what differentiation means to them. In addition, this chapter investigates research on the brain and learning that provides a rationale for differentiating instruction.

Chapter 3: All About the Learners

The Take Away guiding this chapter is "Learning How Student Data Support Differentiation." Chapter 3 addresses the center point of differentiation: the students. In order to differentiate instruction, a PLC's first learner-centered task is to conduct explicit measures to really get to know the students that the team members serve. This chapter examines ways to determine student readiness, student interests, and student learning profiles. We also include basic facts about gender and culture, as well as student attitudes and self-esteem.

Chapter 4: Changing the Content

Shaped by the Take Away "Learning How Teachers Differentiate Content to Meet Student Needs," chapter 4 starts with a practical look at what the process of differentiation actually looks and sounds like in the K–12 classroom. It introduces three proven macrostrategies that teachers can effectively use as they plan how to offer a more differentiated approach to instruction: (1) complexity, (2) resources, and (3) environment.

Chapter 5: Changing the Process

Chapter 5's Take Away is "Learning How Teachers Differentiate Learning Processes to Meet Student Needs." This discussion provides readers with an in-depth look at various techniques to change student learning processes. Chapter 5 presents and analyzes differentiation options in three major areas of development: (1) direct instruction, (2) cooperative learning, and (3) inquiry learning.

Chapter 6: Changing the Product

Guided by the Take Away "Learning How Teachers Differentiate Product Options to Meet Student Needs," chapter 6 investigates specific areas in which teachers can design product options as evidence of student learning. Embedded in this differentiation theory of changing the product is the understanding that students thrive when teachers give them multiple entry points, exit points, and accountability options.

Chapter 7: Diverse-Learner Strategies

Chapter 7 is directed by the Take Away "Learning How PLCs Share Differentiation Strategies for Diverse Learners." This chapter explores what many teachers are already doing as they address the needs of a diverse classroom culture. Using the concept of learner archetypes, we address the following four types of learners: (1) developing learners, (2) advanced learners, (3) English learners, and (4) learners with special needs.

Chapter 8: Changing Lessons for Student Success

This chapter's Take Away is "Learning How Teachers Move Differentiated Lessons From Theory to Practice." The discussion helps PLC teams focus on applying the differentiation principles of change, challenge, and choice to lesson design. Chapter 8 guides teachers as they apply the tenets of the Tomlinson model of differentiated instruction, using a step-by-step process of changing the content, the processes, and the products to address student readiness levels, interests, and learning profiles. The chapter includes sample lessons at the elementary, middle, and high school levels.

Chapter 9: Changing Units for Student Success

Highlighting the Take Away "Learning How Teachers Move Differentiated Curriculum Units From Theory to Practice," chapter 9 provides tools to differentiate the curriculum unit. Teachers change the products by offering multimodal entry points and exit points, and they change accountability by offering multiple assessment options in the areas of traditional portfolios and performance. The chapter also includes curriculum units at the elementary, middle, and high school levels.

Chapter 10: Next Steps

The Take Away for chapter 10 is "Learning How Teachers Decide on the Next Student-Success Priority," which emphasizes the importance of using data when considering what the next steps are. Chapter 10 focuses team members on specifically what they will do to implement continual instructional change in their classrooms. Examples of a semester-long schedule and yearlong schedule are included to guide teams.

Action Options

It is time to look at the first Action Options section. Start by revisiting the Take Away objective, read the introductory comment on the connections to learning communities, and proceed to the specific Action Option strategies. This section differs from other Action Option sections you will encounter because it addresses two separate Take Aways with two Action Options each.

> **PLC TAKE AWAY**
> Learning How Collaboration Supports Substantive Change

PLC teams consist of classroom teachers who have had their schedules modified to provide time to plan together. Unfortunately, busy teachers may initially treat this time as a bother rather than a benefit. One key to helping teachers value this collaborative planning time is the use of structured, interactive strategies by PLC leaders. Cooperative structures are familiar instructional tools to teachers; when used within the culture of PLC-team discussions, these tools provide a comfort zone for interacting with others. This approach takes away some of the discomfort of leading the group, since teacher leaders rotate through the leadership role.

Providing structures for collaborative conversations is one of the most critical elements of PLCs. These structures quickly become part of the PLC norms and provide the tools for productive discourse. In addition, another benefit of using interactive strategies to foster collegial conversations is the opportunity for participants to transfer these engaging strategies to their own classrooms.

Following are two collaborative, team-building Action Options: (1) the Human Graph and (2) the AB Pyramid Game. In addition, the All Things PLC website (www.allthingsplc.info) is important to note early in this discussion. This site provides a plethora of resource options for PLCs to reference as their work unfolds and includes articles, blogs, conversations, threaded discussions, and success stories from school staff across North America.

Action Option 1: Human Graph

One consistent feature of any high-performing group is that all members work together toward a common goal. Before that can happen, however, the group has to have a clear understanding of where they are in relation to the goals of the group.

The Human Graph is an effective way to determine where the group stands while simultaneously giving feedback to every group member. In this way, the whole staff can see how other members of the PLC feel about the progress of their team. The focus topic for this Human Graph is *Our PLC team is . . .*

To begin, designate five spots in the front of the room, like the baseline of a bar graph, and label them with the following headings:

1 Fishing for PLC ideas

2 Forming PLC teams

3 Floundering in team meetings

4 Functioning as a PLC team

5 Flourishing as a PLC team

Ask participants to stand on the line they feel best describes where their PLC is in terms of development. Encourage them to have a conversation with those on the same line, explaining and justifying why they selected that position. Do not spend too much time defining the terms on the graph. Tell participants that the vagueness is intentional as it makes the activity more engaging. It requires them to make inferences and value judgments.

After a sufficient amount of time, sample the various opinions of the group. Allow people to change their positions as they hear ideas that make them question their original decisions. It's okay for them to change their minds. By allowing people to share their thinking, the whole group becomes aware of members' opinions on the PLC's progress.

A benefit of using the Human Graph activity, rather than just having a discussion around a table, is that it forces members to vote with their feet. This act of taking a stand communicates what they feel in a concrete way that is clear to the group as a whole. If the goal is to determine how the PLC members feel about their team progress, the Human Graph is a more active and engaging method than a discussion or member survey.

Following is a possible Human Graph application for new teams. Begin by saying that a PLC focuses on these five elements:

1 Students

2 Results

3 Lifelong learning

4 Common values

5 Shared vision/mission

Ask the participants to stand on the attribute they feel is the most important. Urge them to discuss their thinking with others who have chosen the same attribute. This simple strategy elicits valuable feedback in a very short period of time because members see where they are in relation to the rest of the group and are able to discuss their positions.

After processing the results of the graph, the members of the PLC can offer suggestions on how they might use the Human Graph in their individual classrooms.

Action Option 2: AB Pyramid Game

The AB Pyramid Game stirs up prior knowledge and introduces vocabulary around the idea of professional learning communities. This game is also effective for PLC team building.

To begin, one member of the PLC team facilitates the AB Pyramid Game while the rest of the members split into pairs; each pair sits shoulder to shoulder, with one person facing a screen and the other with his or her back to the screen.

The facilitator puts a single PLC vocabulary word on the screen, and the members facing the screen give one-word clues to their partners to help them guess the words. Each participant should have two rounds as the giver of clues and two rounds as the guesser. This role reversal increases the emotional hook as the teacher teams begin to understand how to play the game. When a participant correctly guesses a word, the partner giving clues signals the facilitator by raising his or her hand. The facilitator then shows the next word on the screen. This approach ensures good pacing for the whole group—both for partners who guessed correctly and quickly and for partners who are stuck. For each of the four rounds, one member will try to get his or her partner to guess four PLC vocabulary words:

Round 1—*collaboration, team, data, results*

Round 2—*inquiry, assessments, together, success*

Round 3—*mission, measurable, structure, help*

Round 4—*goal, learning, formative, colleagues*

Once the four words in that round have been guessed, and before beginning the next round, the facilitator has the whole group look at the four words from the previous round and talk briefly about their relevance to professional learning communities. Then, the partners switch chairs and viewing positions for the next round. This process continues for four rounds, until all four sets of words have been used.

The AB Pyramid Game works well for new PLCs or if there has been staff turnover. This activity is an effective way to re-establish the meaning of PLCs and the work they do. It is a quick review of terms and concepts.

While this game seems a bit frivolous to some, team building within PLC groups cannot be emphasized enough. Teams begin to function smoothly when team members get to know and feel comfortable with one another.

The AB Pyramid Game, as with all of the Action Options, can be easily adapted to classroom content and transferred to engaging applications for students. It works well, of course, with vocabulary for various subject matters. In addition, it can be used to emphasize concepts and skills. For example, teachers can use it to unpack concepts such as *photosynthesis* or *democracy*. Others can use it to develop mathematics skills; for instance, consider a teacher projecting the number 49. The viewer states number combinations that equal 49, such as 24 + 25, while the guesser identifies the answer. This activity can also be used to develop foreign language skills; for example, the viewer would translate the Spanish word on-screen into English, and the guesser would then translate the word back into Spanish.

PLC TAKE AWAY
Learning How PLCs Use This Resource to Promote Student Success

Two Action Options for this PLC Take Away include the Rank and Tally activity and the Skim and Scan activity.

Rank and Tally gives voice to each and every member of the professional learning community as they decide on the most helpful way to use this book to guide their differentiation work. With student success as the primary goal, supported by the spirit and culture of the learning community, this activity is the perfect opportunity to hear all the opinions and ideas of the membership.

The Skim and Scan activity gives members enough preliminary information about a resource to question and comment on the preferred path for initiating a more explicit approach to differentiating instruction.

Action Option 1: Rank and Tally

First, members should list the specific options that their PLC teams are considering. In this example, we will look at possible next steps for PLC teams in terms of using this resource to their best advantage.

Options for using *Supporting Differentiated Instruction* as a PLC resource for differentiated instruction include:

- Do a PLC book study.
- Jump into a specific chapter.
- Jigsaw chapters for quick overview.
- Read individually, dialogue with a partner.
- Do a combination of the above.

Instruct PLC members to individually rank the five options according to their preferences. Then, as a team-building exercise, ask members to predict which option will be the highest ranked and to discuss their rationale. Finally, take a tally by having members vote for one of the two top-ranked items. The option with the highest score is the one that the PLC team agrees to pursue, after some discussion about how the strategy will work. This simple rank-and-tally strategy helps PLC team members reach a decision quickly, with input from all.

At the same time, it models a strategy that has classroom implications. Teachers can use Rank and Tally with students as they weigh in on various ideas. For example, they can rank the characters in a story according to who they relate to most, or they can rank the simple machines by frequency of use in their lives. Once the students have ranked the items, the teacher can tally the totals to show the big picture—the overall view of the class. It is a powerful higher-order thinking activity that helps kids evaluate and make judgments.

Action Option 2: Skim and Scan

A simple skim of the table of contents gives PLC teams fertile ground for discussion, and it may help them decide how to best use *Supporting Differentiated Instruction*. This tried-and-true strategy that teachers urge students to try when they preview a book also serves PLC teams well.

Learning communities focus on anything teachers might do to ensure student success. Some of these simple tools, when used by PLC teams, prompt teachers to take them right back to their classrooms. When PLC teacher leaders model engaging learning, they foster the concept of an adult learning community.

CHAPTER 1

ALL ABOUT COLLABORATION

PLC TAKE AWAY

Learning How PLCs Support Student Success

When addressing the question of how professional learning communities support student success, two aspects are important to discuss. The first concerns the students' needs, and the second, the teacher's role. Addressing student needs turns the focus of education to the one and only mission that matters: the unequivocal success of the students served. That is what schooling is about—the vision, the goal, and the mission! When student success becomes the only thing schools focus on, the path becomes clear. Schools must find ways to harness the power of the faculty in service of students.

If student success is the sole purpose of our schooling systems, it requires unprecedented measures. It dictates actions that consolidate the power of the teaching staff in ways that allow them to impact each and every student that passes through the hallways of their schools. How do teachers rally to this cause? How do teachers accept and carry the burden they have been given when the goal is strictly related to the success of the student?

Schools around the world have embraced this vision of corralling teacher resources to meet student needs. Documented by many (Darling-Hammond, 2009; DuFour & Eaker, 1998; Hord & Sommers, 2009), shared leadership through professional collaborations is an idea whose time has arrived. Teaching as a private endeavor (Joyce & Showers, 2002) is no longer compatible with the behavior of an effective teacher. Teachers aren't expected to enter their classrooms, close the doors, and do what they do. The model has changed.

Embodying the PLC principles of collaboration, interdependence, and a focus on students eventually and inevitably causes the incredible shift that occurs in the far-reaching goals of these schools. The professional teams within these learning communities understand, accept, and pursue a laser-beam focus on ensuring student success.

Guiding Principles

In brief, a professional learning community is formally defined by the leading voices in the field as

> educators committed to working collaboratively in ongoing processes of collective inquiry and action research to achieve better results for the students they serve. Professional learning communities operate under the assumption that the key to improved learning for students is continuous job-embedded learning for educators. (DuFour, DuFour, Eaker, & Many, 2006, p. 217)

The key to a successful PLC is captured in three big ideas: (1) focus on learning, (2) focus on collaborative culture, and (3) focus on results (DuFour, DuFour, & Eaker, 2008).

Focus on Learning

The biggest idea of all—a focus on and a commitment to the learning of each student—speaks most directly to the clear purpose of PLCs. This idea is epitomized in the questions that structure PLC work (DuFour et al., 2008): What do we want the students to learn? How will we know that they know it? What we will do when they don't? Or do?

These are simple questions, yet they hold profound wisdom. When teachers—working collaboratively and conversing professionally—determine the complex answers, the school is on its way to true north. When teaching teams structure their learning community in a way that allows them to do their work, and when they are able to function efficiently and effectively for the welfare and fulfillment of the learners, then the PLCs optimize their work.

As the PLC teams pass through the early stages, filled with doubt and challenge, to more mature stages of confidence and purpose, a shift occurs in their culture and in their spirit, and the focus is set firmly and foundationally on student learning. Members come together to define what the PLC and the PLC teams must do to ensure students success, commit to continual learning as professionals, and focus on data-driven results. It is the beginning of a collaborative process that impacts how the school moves forward toward student success.

Focus on Collaborative Culture

The second tenet that guides the work of the PLCs defines the very nature of the professional communities. Collaboration begins when teams are formed, time is provided, beliefs are examined, and expectations are clear. While this collaboration is often awkward at first, and barely yields agreements that can actually be acted upon, these early gatherings set the climate for sharing ideas in the first of many collegial conversations.

Over time, and with specific shared beliefs intact, teams gradually sense a cultural change that binds them. The attitudes and behaviors of the team members change as they reflect on their roles as professionals with responsibilities not only to student learning, but also to their own learning. They demonstrate a spirit of commitment to continual learning, to reflective practice, and to the vision and mission of authentic, student-centered schooling.

One final clarification: PLCs are not the meetings. Rather, the meetings are the glue that holds the learning communities together and the catalyst for brewing significant change. These meetings become microcosms of collaborative culture as the PLC teams learn to act in synchronicity.

Focus on Results

Measurable, data-driven results reign supreme in the third and final precept of PLCs. Whatever the work of PLC teams—from aligning standards and writing common assessments to implementing the pyramid of interventions—the final outcome is about visible, measurable, provable results in the performance of the student and in the person that student is becoming.

All PLC stakeholders soon learn that a PLC is not about intentions; rather, it is about results. Stakeholders then receive consistent and continual feedback on the progress they are making. They understand and embrace the power of data and information as the means to determine policy, practices, and programs. This fidelity to feedback drives the work of PLCs and keeps them on target for improving student learning.

Through this dedication to data, PLCs target what students need to know and how teachers know when they know it. The assessments reveal the gaps in learning and indicate which students need instructional interventions. Once the data are clear, teams concentrate on how to differentiate instruction via interventions that will work for a range of student needs. The concept of differentiation takes root, and teachers consider various instructional methodologies.

Accepting these precepts as the premise of this discussion, we turn attention to the foundational decisions that school leaders must manage as they begin and form their teams within PLCs. With the definition of professional learning communities in hand, teams invariably ask basic questions about the process, which include important logistical concerns.

Why Are PLCs Formed?

This is perhaps the most intriguing question to teachers who have worked in virtual isolation most of their careers. Teachers aren't sure what the explicit purpose is for forming teams or developing the culture of a PLC, other than providing an opportunity to meet and talk. Based on past experiences with "talk time," many teachers don't see this as a priority in their busy schedules. So, why are PLCs forming in schools across North America and around the world?

As mentioned previously, the primary and overriding purpose of PLCs is to foster collaborative, professional conversations around the topic of ensuring student success.

Ensuring student success means putting in place, with the full consensus and commitment of the PLCs, a no-fail system with checklists and checkpoints. PLCs, when working well, do whatever it takes to close the achievement gap (DuFour et al., 2008) in order to make certain no student falls through cracks in the system.

Schools committed to creating and acting within the culture and spirit of PLCs employ multiple measures, such as a pyramid of interventions, to ensure that they are supporting all students for their utmost success in the system. A school's support systems might include programs such as Freshman Academy, Counselor Watch, Peer Mediation, Guided Study Program, and Case Study Evaluation (DuFour et al., 2008). While each district or school designs its own pyramid of interventions to ensure student learning, this all-encompassing, student-focused goal is the ultimate answer to why schools form PLCs.

Who Is on a PLC Team?

Some of the most pressing questions that plague the early talks within the PLC often center on the basic decision of who is on what PLC team and why. The questions range from who decides to what the best grouping of teachers will do.

On examination of these, a whole cluster of other questions bubbles up: Who will be in my group? How many of us will there be? What will we have in common? Do I have any options in the process of selection? While these are highly personal concerns about the change to come, some critical factors can help school leaders make the appropriate decisions for their unique set of circumstances.

In fact, many kinds of PLC groupings exist, including grade-level teams, departmental teams, and vertical teams spanning different grade levels; teams focused on particular instructional initiatives, such as differentiated instruction, cooperative learning, or technology integration; and, finally, core teaching teams at middle schools. Of course, these grouping decisions center on conceptual goals of the district or school as well as the practicalities of size, space, and demographics.

Team assignment is a critical juncture for professional learning communities that are just starting. While most PLC teams find their common ground over time, the composition of the group may well make or break a successful team launch. The actual determination of the group composition is usually in the hands of the building administrator or a building leadership team. In some cases, however, faculty members have valid input about the formation of their PLC's teams. A brief look at the various compositions of groups and the pros and cons of each follows.

Grade-Level PLCs

Grade-level teams are logical groupings for PLCs. A plus is that teachers can share content concerns that target a particular set of students. This means they must address the concerns about what they want students to know, how to recognize if they know it, and what they will do if students do or don't know it. A minus is that the team may focus more on the curriculum rather than on students. Small schools may prefer a different kind of PLC grouping because they have too few teachers at a given grade level. Similarly, large schools may have too many teachers at the various levels to make it an efficient or effective grouping model.

Departmental PLCs

Departmental teams make sense on the surface because teachers are experts in their subject matters; this facilitates curricular work on essential standards and common assessments. Departmental teams tend to be content-focused, and that focus may override putting student talents and needs first. Also, smaller buildings may not have enough faculty for departmental PLCs.

Vertical PLCs

Vertical teams span several grade levels, specifically across a particular content area, so that teachers can compare what is being taught at one level to what is needed at the next. The advantages are the platform for articulation across grade levels and the tendency to move away from a curricular orientation to a more student-centered one. In addition, the vertical teams might work well in small schools that have fewer staff members at the various grade levels. One disadvantage may be in the availability of times to meet as schedules often cluster around grade levels.

Task Force PLCs

The PLC teams formed around a school task force, such as restructuring the report card or moving the staff and students to the small schools concept, can be powerful. In these instances, the PLCs become agents of substantive change that may lead the school to cultural changes that epitomize PLCs. Yet the real challenge with these kinds of PLCs is that they are not really focused directly on students, but rather on micro- and macrochanges that often impact students in a future setting. Their concerns may not be connected to the day-to-day success of students. However, these PLC teams often last far beyond the initial task-force initiative and can be the seeds of development.

Professional Development PLCs

One interesting PLC team composition is to assign teachers to, or have teachers choose, a professional development focus. For example, teachers might select the differentiation PLC team, the formative assessment PLC team, or the integrated technology PLC team based on interest and relevancy. In this way, the district or school builds its site capacity by creating experts in the various professional development areas. This can be quite effective in some districts; however, this PLC model does not always have the student contact that might be needed to impact students more directly.

Core Team PLCs

The middle school core team of teachers is a perfect PLC grouping because of their responsibilities to the same student "family" or "house." While these middle school teachers may still meet as departmental teams, the core teams usually take precedent with middle school PLCs. Any concern with this grouping for PLCs may lie in breaking old team habits about how they function in meetings.

By considering the possible team models, staff and leaders have an opportunity for rich discussion and robust decision making—coveted collaborative skills of highly functioning PLC teams.

PLCs must remember to address not only the composition of the groups, but also the ideal number of people in each group. For the sake of expediency and efficiency, it is best, in our opinion, to form PLC teams with four to six members. With smaller teams, it is easier to schedule regular time together that will yield maximum attendance for the meetings. As a side note, the work must go on regardless of who is at the meeting; otherwise, the team misses important decisions and deadlines and may become bogged down with unfinished business.

In regard to the concern about who decides on the composition of PLC teams, a tradition has emerged. The lead administrator usually determines teams with input solicited from the school improvement team, grade-level leaders, or department heads. Or the administrator may create a selection committee. The main point is to decide how to decide and to follow through.

What Do PLCs Do?

Through collegial conversation, the setting of agreed-upon goals, continuous inquiry through action research, data-driven decisions, and adherence to and evidence of results, PLC teams do whatever it takes to ensure the success of the students they serve. While the philosophy and actions are intertwined, it seems appropriate at this juncture to elaborate further on what the PLCs and the teams that work within them actually do.

Collegial Conversations

Collegial conversations drive the work of PLCs. Through team-building activities, as well as through the natural camaraderie that occurs as people work together on common tasks, a trusting environment gradually evolves. This trust between team members is essential as the work continues. This team effort manifests the culture of interdependence in the school PLC as a whole. Team members who understand that the conversations, debates, and decisions should focus on pertinent educational concerns manage the issues that arise in highly professional ways. That steady level of professionalism is key to the efforts of the ever-evolving, ever-changing learning communities.

Goal Setting

Goal setting is the pivotal force behind learning communities. PLCs work from carefully crafted, clearly articulated student learning goals. Within the PLC teams, these highly honored goals map the expected results. The goals provide the framework for seeking success and prepare the team for the action details to follow. The synergy of having everyone agree to the goal propels the remaining work.

Continuous Inquiry

PLCs also use continuous inquiry through ongoing action research. This inquiry is at the heart of team discussions; it helps members clarify the goals and the subsequent actions. PLCs and PLC teams design intentional ways of examining practices that promote student learning for their collective or respective classrooms. By investigating issues and concerns within the parameters of accepted research models, teachers engage in observation and evaluation processes. For example, PLCs may enact a research project on the observable differences in student learning when students work alone as compared to when they work collaboratively. Action research lies at the core of substantive changes teams make in instruction.

Data-Driven Decisions

Inextricably linked to that inquiry is the role that data play before, during, and after the learning occurs. Data serve as the foundation of the collegial conversations that take place within team meetings. Baseline data provide the information teachers use in terms of student placement in courses and within the classes. Formative data obtained during actual instruction and common assessments are the tools that PLCs use to check for understanding and determine next steps.

Data are the lifeline of PLCs and the catalyst for their decision-making process, regardless of whether the data are observational, anecdotal, checklisted, recorded electronically, reported graphically, quantitative, qualitative, soft data that tell the backstory, or hard data that bare the facts. Data reveal the results of the instruction and interventions.

Results

By reading and reviewing results, PLCs obtain the proper input to move forward. When the results are in, the analysis begins. And the results arrive throughout the term, not just at the end or after the annual testing regimen. Teams garner results through regularly scheduled data-gathering measures that, in turn, guide the collegial conversations of PLCs. Data collection is hard work that dictates persistence and precision over and over again; this adherence to periodic data checks creates a results-driven climate that energizes the teams.

When Do PLC Teams Do Their Collaborative Work?

While the next two questions, when and where do PLC teams meet to do their collaborative work, have fairly straightforward answers, the teams often need time and resources to sort them out. Researchers and writers in the field (DuFour et al., 2008) argue that professional learning communities are integral to teachers' professional collaborations, and that regularly scheduled weekly meetings are best when woven into the staff schedules. While scheduling is admittedly a tedious and complex task, particularly for larger school systems, the schedule itself is also a mirror that reflects the principles and priorities of the system. At the risk of simplifying this issue, we frequently recommend that teams meet once a week, during the workday, for a minimum of one hour. That leads to a related concern: where do PLCs meet?

Where Do PLC Teams Meet?

Learning communities often assemble wherever space is available that is convenient for the individual members. The only real constraints, other than availability, are that the location be in the building—as central as possible to the various teachers—and afford some level of privacy, mobility, and interactivity.

While a permanent locale for meeting is probably better, some teams find it helpful and even enlightening to rotate among the various teachers' classrooms. This does allow members to gain a certain perspective as they have the opportunity to be immersed in the culture of various classrooms. It is always an eye-opening experience for teachers to get inside another teacher's classroom and see the visible evidence of instruction. However, the stability and familiarity offered by meeting at the same place every time has many advantages for the work PLCs do. For example, educators will have their materials, they know where they are going each time, and they have their routines in place.

How Do PLCs and PLC Teams Function?

The final question is the most practical. Once the school forms teams and designates meeting times and places, how do teachers within PLCs learn to function as a collaborative team, and how can they make their teams skillful, effective, and focused on student success?

The answer lies in the very deliberate structures put in place from day one. Learning communities need organizing structures, discussion structures, mediation structures, and evaluation structures within the teams. By *structures*, we mean norms and heuristics to guide effective meeting times, as well as rules and rights that follow the decisions made in the PLC team planning and follow-up sessions.

Setting simple norms is often the first order of business. Commonly agreed-upon norms frame the processes that facilitate the meetings and the work itself. For example, PLC team norms might include the following:

- Starting and ending on time
- Rotating PLC leadership every month
- Requiring active participation by each member
- Deciding by consensus
- Listing action steps at every meeting

Hands-on learning is an expectation of PLCs. By name and nature, PLCs are learning organizations. They are open to learning by trial and error and understand that the structures are somewhat loosely defined, providing room for changes, modifications, and adjustments as the teams find the structures, norms, and work ethic that work best for them. In fact, each PLC team may have slightly different sets of norms, tailored over time. For example, a conference attendee sharing ideas said, "The meeting officially begins three minutes after the start time." This team's members found that they needed a few minutes to chat and get settled in before they could proceed effectively with their agenda. While they wanted to have a transition period, they realized that an hour is not much time, so they needed to get down to business as quickly as possible.

Just as the norms guide the work of PLC team meetings, rules and rights may be used to guide reactions to instructional interventions. Rules set needed parameters. For example, the instruction and intervention rules might include the following:

- Propose data-driven interventions.
- Pilot interventions to test the idea for early results.
- Monitor program interventions regularly.

While these are the kinds of rules that ensure a focus on learning and results, they also help PLC members in their decision-making process because they limit the process in healthy and effective ways.

In addition, certain rights accompany the work of the PLC. These provide individual members with a voice that, at times, may need a forum for dissent. Rights might include the following:

- Each member has an equal voice.
- Each member has an equal vote.
- Each member has an equal responsibility.

All of these structures—including meeting protocols, evolving heuristics, instruction and intervention rules, and member rights—truly support the PLC journey.

PLCs and Differentiation

Because *Supporting Differentiated Instruction* is a guide to implement and support differentiation using a PLC approach, let's make clear the connection between the PLC and differentiation. Teams functioning well within a PLC focus on what the students need in order to reach their potential. The purpose of this resource is to give the members of those collaborative teams ideas about how to better reach these students.

Differentiation serves as the instructional umbrella for the kinds of decisions team members make to tap into the talents and needs of students. It is the overriding concept that dictates attention to what students need to know, and it continues to guide teachers as they consider what to do when the students know or don't know it. We've designed the following chapters to help team members examine not just what they are going to teach, but how they are going to teach it.

Action Options

> **PLC TAKE AWAY**
>
> Learning How PLCs Support Student Success

While it may be easy to create a list of dos and don'ts, it's much harder to genuinely agree on, and adhere to, norms that ultimately serve the goals of the PLCs. The philosophy behind the creation of PLCs is that schools can't keep doing things the same way they've been doing them in past; teachers have to come together and make student achievement the number-one priority. Thus, it would be the height of irony if the rules and norms created by PLCs were for something other than to ensure the success of the PLC's mission. As teachers learn to embrace this idea, learning communities develop into productive, mature learning organizations.

The Action Options in this chapter include ways to establish norms for the PLC and the PLC teams. The T-Chart activity facilitates a preliminary discussion. A second discussion facilitator is the Web of Concerns, which results in prioritized agenda items. In addition, visit www.allthingsplc.info/tools/samples.php to read inspirational PLC stories.

Action Option 1: The T-Chart

Basic courtesy rules, such as "Start on time and end on time," can be adopted by members without much discussion. Coming up with rules of operation may take more time, but the energy spent on these will serve multiple purposes and will lead to more successful PLCs.

To define and refine basic rules of operation, use the T-Chart activity to deconstruct norms. Randomly pick a facilitator for the day, for instance, the one whose birthday is soonest. Draw a T-Chart on the board with two options: *Looks Like* and *Sounds Like* (see fig. 1.1, page 22). (See page 25 for a reproducible of this chart. Visit **go.solution-tree.com/instruction** to download all reproducibles in this book.)

The facilitator's job is to elicit ideas for working in the PLC team, help specify behaviors that will facilitate the team's work, and transform these statements into agreed-upon norms. For example, when discussing the rule of respecting others, one member may describe it as, "Honoring the comments of all PLC members." The facilitator then asks members to talk with a partner about what honoring comments looks like. "Respect" would not be the appropriate answer. Respect is an abstract idea that sounds good, yet is hard to put into action. A better response describes how respect looks in action. For example, "Making eye contact with the speaker" is an example of what it would look like to honor the comments of all PLC members. The facilitator summarizes, puts this on the left side of the T-Chart, and continues until there are four or five examples.

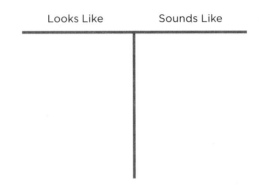

Figure 1.1: Sample t-chart.

This process is repeated on the right side of the T-Chart: "Sounds Like." Accepted suggestions should be specific and clear. For instance, "polite and professional" does not answer "What does it sound like to honor the comments from all PLC members?" A better answer would be: "It sounds like, 'That's a great comment' or 'Good idea' or 'That makes perfect sense.'" These comments of acknowledgment say what they mean.

Covering issues like basic group dynamics may seem rudimentary, but teams should tackle these early to ensure more productive and collegial sessions. Using the T-Chart activity to discuss and clarify behavior expectations will make the norms operational, which will serve the long-term goals of the PLC. This initial conversation, with a focus on creating and honoring norms that count, helps PLCs and their teams develop and mature as learning communities. With respectful and professional norms in place, and with input from each member, PLC teams can move from internal concerns to the real concerns of student achievement, goals, and common assessments.

In addition, the T-Chart strategy can easily be transferred to the classroom. Examples of classroom applications for the T-Chart include: What does a good thinker look like and sound like? What does a scientist look like and sound like? What does a friendship look like and sound like?

Teachers are probably the most pragmatic of all adult learners. They want their time to be well spent, so whenever they can learn a new strategy while engaged in the process of the PLC team's work, they benefit.

Action Option 2: Web of Concerns

PLCs are effective when they focus on the success of students. When PLC teams spend too much time lamenting the role of public education in national, provincial, or state policies, they may steer off their desired course. If these issues cannot be changed or improved directly by the members of the PLCs, then the valuable time together is best spent improving student achievement. The PLC is not a forum to establish what *can't* be done, but rather an opportunity to focus on what *can* be done and how to accomplish it. Setting an agenda of topics, concerns, and suggestions generated by PLC members is a powerful step toward dealing with these issues successfully. While members of the PLC team may think there is agreement on what needs to be done to improve the classroom instruction and increase student achievement, members often have very different ideas about the priorities.

The Web of Concerns, a graphic organizer, defines the attributes of the topic in a visible way. The web focuses thinking inward toward defining the concern. Use the Web of Concerns as a way to expose the issues and to set the agenda. Students should always be the focus when teams set priorities. It's that simple. Also, understand that the Web of Concerns may generate items that need several meeting agendas to address.

To create a Web of Concerns, the facilitator draws a circle on the whiteboard, with a target phrase in the center, for example, *Ninth-grade concerns* (see fig. 1.2, page 24). Members then contribute their thoughts to the conversation, and the leader records key words as lines or spokes stemming out from the edge of the circle, creating a web of ideas. Some spokes for this concern might be: *tardiness, essay writing, math scores, male reading scores, homework, parent involvement,* and *hall behavior.* Once the Web of Concerns is complete, the team prioritizes the concerns. These rankings may take many forms, but some helpful categories include: *immediate action, action, needs study,* and *combine.* This Web of Concerns often leads to the team agenda for the next few months.

Teachers can easily use the Web of Concerns in classroom activities. They may delineate the attributes of a character in a language arts story, the resources of a region in social studies, or the characteristics of a mammal in science class. It provides a powerful graphic organizer that makes the thinking visible to all.

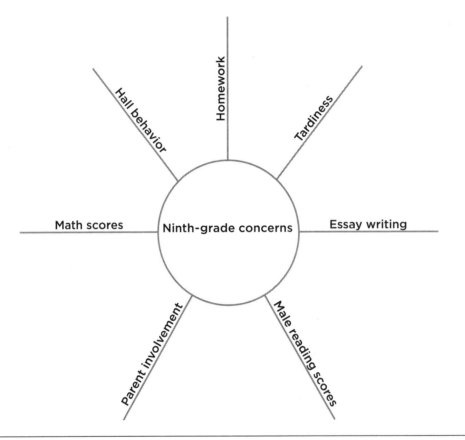

Figure 1.2: Sample web of concerns.

T-Chart

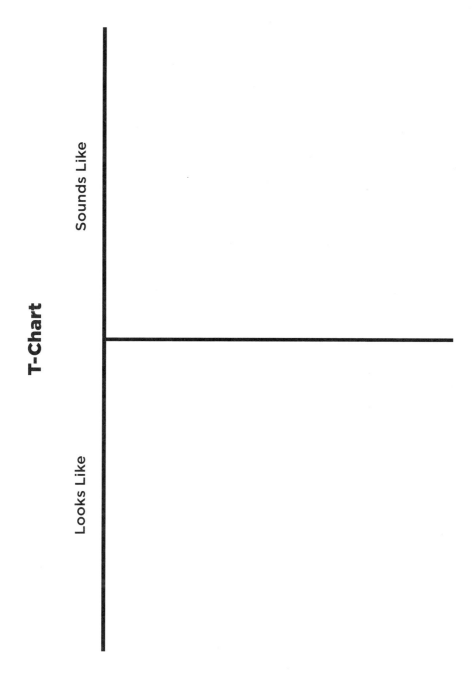

Sounds Like

Looks Like

CHAPTER **2**

ALL ABOUT DIFFERENTIATION

> **PLC TAKE AWAY**
>
> Learning How Differentiation Addresses Student Needs

This chapter defines, describes, and delineates the complex concept of differentiation as applied to student learning. While chapter 1 explained PLCs—the first of the two core concepts of the text—differentiation now takes center stage.

First, we present the research rationale for differentiation, which shows that differentiation follows what brain science calls for—a different approach for each person. Second, we discuss the concept of school change (Fullan & Stiegelbauer, 1991) as a part of professional development (Guskey, 2000) and how it relates to the work of differentiation in a team atmosphere. Third, we define the theory of differentiation based on the work of a lead researcher and writer in the field, Carol Ann Tomlinson (2005), as well as based on classroom experiences that demonstrate the theory in practice. Fourth, we delineate the three principles of differentiation. In the final section, we explore the role of data in differentiation. In embracing the practice of differentiated instruction, it becomes clearer why and how PLCs play a key role in supporting that practice.

The remaining chapters of *Supporting Differentiated Instruction* unpack the process of change toward more differentiated instruction through the support, culture, and work of PLC teams.

Research Rationale for Differentiation

Based on the meta-analysis by Caine, Caine, McClintic, and Klimek (2009), we've distilled the research on the brain and learning into the following twelve critical points:

1. Learning is enhanced by challenge and inhibited by threat.

2. Emotions are critical to patterning.

3. Learning involves both focused attention and peripheral perception.

4. The brain has a spatial memory system and a set of systems for rote learning.

5. The brain processes parts and wholes simultaneously.

6. Learning engages the entire physiology.

7. The brain is a parallel processor.

8. Learning is embedded in natural and social settings.

9. Each brain is unique.

10. The search for meaning is innate.

11. The search for meaning occurs through patterning.

12. Learning always involves conscious and unconscious processes. (Pete & Fogarty, 2007, pp. viii–ix)

These points provide a rich philosophical foundation for differentiating instruction. They guide the everyday decisions teachers make about instructional input, student groupings, curricular designs, and the range of assessments used in classrooms today.

According to Carol Ann Tomlinson (1999a), the need for emotional safety, appropriate challenge, and self-constructed meaning suggests that a one-size-fits-all approach to classroom teaching is ineffective for most students and harmful to some. In order to create meaning in each individual brain, learners need many entryways to make sense of the world around them. They need a brain-friendly classroom in which instruction is varied, diversified, and differentiated. Because differentiation provides this variation, it fully supports the uniqueness of every brain.

Fullan's Theory of Change

The change to differentiation may sound intimidating for individual teachers, but within a PLC, teams can move forward together in an effective, sustained way. Michael Fullan presents the process of change in three distinct, yet blended phases:

1 Initiate the change.

2 Implement the change.

3 Institutionalize the change.

Initiate the Change

In the first phase, initiation, the idea or innovation is introduced, unpacked, and highly publicized for the sake of the constituents involved. The goal is to get the word out with a basic level of understanding of the theory and rationale behind differentiation and to begin the move of stakeholders toward implementation of the new practices in their classrooms (Fullan & Stiegelbauer, 1991).

Implement the Change

In traditional change models, as the innovation moves into implementation, the adage "Go with ones ready to go" is often the starting point. Starting implementation with its supporters gives the innovation a strong start; motivated teachers energize the initiative along the way. However, in many situations, teachers are burned out by the extensive initiation phase and never actually arrive at the implementation phase.

This is where PLCs come in. PLC teams—armed and ready with the initial information and training—form a support mechanism to encourage and coach all of the teachers in their early efforts at implementation. Change is no longer a singular effort. In fact, the PLC-supported change model adheres to the proven progression of professional development that Guskey (2000) discusses:

1 Change introduced with professional development

2 Change in practice

3 Change in student achievement

4 Change in beliefs

Change seems to encompass a predictable path, according to this research. Following a professional learning experience, teachers who practice the initiative begin to see significant, observable changes in their students' efforts and achievements. As this happens, teachers begin to question their usual methods of instruction and start embracing the new ideas with the enthusiasm, energy, and commitment needed to see the implementation through to the final phase: institutionalization. All teachers benefit in the PLC team–supported model, because as they converse, coach, and teach one another, their own learning deepens.

Institutionalize the Change

This final phase, institutionalizing the initiative, occurs over time. An institutionalized instructional practice is one that has become part of the culture, curriculum, and policy of the school. The PLC holds all stakeholders accountable for using the practice and the learning it supports. An institutionalized initiative encompasses the best practices in professional learning (Fogarty & Pete, 2007a), including the following:

- Sustained over time—a three- to five-year plan
- Job-embedded—meetings built into the workday
- Collegial—community of learners
- Interactive—goals supported in every way
- Integrated—action-oriented conversations
- Practical—relevant ideas to use immediately
- Results-oriented—evidence of learning

In light of the information in chapter 1, which distilled the guiding principles of PLCs and PLC teams, it is clear how these very same principles—focus on learning, focus on collaborative culture, and focus on results—guide the differentiation process. We now turn to differentiated instruction—first by looking at the definition and theory according to researchers (Tomlinson, 1999a) and then at the experience-based definition by practitioners.

Differentiation Theory: A Research-Based Approach

The term *differentiation* has its roots in gifted education. In the early 1980s, there was a parent outcry to address the needs of students who were considered gifted and talented. While the identification of gifted and talented remains an imperfect science that causes much concern in districts, the identification process originally screened for several areas of giftedness: high intellectual abilities or high intelligence quotient (IQ); high achievement abilities in a specific area such as math; leadership potential; demonstrated talent in the areas of relational skills; visual and performing arts such as music; and creativity or potential for innovative thinking (National Council of Gifted Education, 2008).

However, the identification process became the albatross of the gifted education movement and soon focused solely on high intellectual abilities or high potential in one academic area identified by a triangulated process of IQ scores, achievement test scores, and teacher recommendation.

Once students were identified, "gifted and talented" programs were installed to serve their identified needs, and *differentiation* began to appear in literature and in curricular guidelines. In those early days of gifted education, the federal government and state departments of education called for a gifted-education curriculum that was differentiated from the regular curriculum. In order to qualify for the funding for gifted-and-talented programming, the curriculum had to be distinctly different from the regular curriculum. Thus, gifted curricula developed apart from normal curricular content.

That mandate turned out to be a blessing and a curse. In order to differentiate the curriculum for the gifted and talented, many innovative products and programs emerged on the market. These focused on problem-solving approaches, higher-order thinking, and rich, robust projects that might include, for example, photography, inventions, and civic-oriented campaigns for abolishing graffiti in the community.

While these were highly motivational for the students and provided robust authentic learning experiences, there was an artificial aspect to them. That is, the programs were designed, more often than not, as pull-out programs that were entirely disconnected from the required content of the classroom. These programs did provide a different curriculum that was truly rich and inviting, yet they rarely made real connections between the problem-solving, project-oriented skills that students were learning in the gifted class and the standard curriculum they were learning in their regular classes. That persistent disconnect plagued many who worked in pull-out programs in gifted education. It just didn't make sense.

A leader in the field of differentiation, Carol Ann Tomlinson focused her research at the University of Virginia on gifted education. Her work in that area and in developing the concept of differentiation eventually stretched far beyond her initial focus, however, to define the ways that differentiated instruction would serve the various needs of all students.

Differentiation to Researchers

Differentiation, as defined by Tomlinson and Cunningham Eidson (2003), is a systematic approach to planning curriculum and instruction for academically diverse learners. It is a way of thinking about the classroom with the dual goals of honoring each student's learning needs and maximizing each student's learning capacity. That definition serves the field today as a succinct, yet comprehensive view of differentiation in the classroom.

We have paraphrased similar definitions that shed light on the complex concept of differentiation in the following examples. We extrapolated these examples from ten years of professional development discussions and activities in which teachers worked to define the concept of differentiation:

- Differentiation is classroom practice that looks eye to eye with the reality that kids are different and they learn differently. Effective teachers do whatever it takes to hook the whole range of kids on learning.

- Differentiation is adjusting the teaching process according to the learning needs of the pupils. It can be aimed at a whole class, groups within the class, or individuals.

- Differentiation can be defined as follows:

  - ✚ By task—setting different tasks for pupils of different ability

  - ✚ By outcome—allowing pupil responses at different levels of understanding

  - ✚ By support—giving more help to certain pupils within the group

  - ✚ By expectations—personalizing target goals for students

- Differentiation is a student-centered approach to designing curriculum instruction and assessment to accommodate the learners' needs and talents.

In an effort to define and describe the idea of differentiation, a set of terms often associated with differentiation or differentiated instruction illuminates the concept and process. Among the terms are *personalized, individualized, customized, tailored, tweaked, adjusted, modified, adapted, accommodated, stylized, manipulated,* and *fine-tuned.* Each of these terms captures, to some extent, the essence of differentiation.

What It Is and Isn't

Tomlinson's delineation of what differentiation is and what it isn't provides a richer definition of the term. In her early writings, Tomlinson (2001) says that differentiation is qualitative, student centered, and assessment driven, and is a blend of whole-class, small-group, and individual instruction. She believes it provides multiple approaches to learning, and that it is highly organic.

Tomlinson also writes about what differentiation is not. She states that it is not homogeneous grouping or tracking of students, adjustment of the same lesson, individualized instruction, chaos in the classroom, or louder and slower teaching. We have compiled some of her thoughts in the following feature boxes.

What Differentiation Is!

It is qualitative—adjusting the nature of work, not the quantity of work.

It is student-centered—differing the doorways to learning.

It is assessment driven—assessing for learning and adjusting.

It is whole, small group, and individual—designing effective instruction.

It is a multimodal approach—varying methods of input, process, and output.

It is organic—responding to the dynamics of the interactive classroom.

What Differentiation Is Not!

It is not homogeneous grouping—not tracking, rather forming heterogeneous and mixed-ability groups.

It is not individualized—not trying to do twenty-five different lessons, rather modifying lessons.

It is not chaos—not losing control of classroom, rather employing skillful management.

It is not louder and slower—not doing the same thing again, rather creating a substantive change.

Source: Tomlinson, 2001

In another look at the research-based approach to defining and describing differentiated instruction, Tomlinson uses a telling metaphor. She describes differentiation as not just "tailoring the same suit of clothes." She says, "Trying to stretch a garment that is far too small, or attempting to tuck and gather a garment that is far too large, is likely to be less effective than getting clothes that are the right fit at a given time" (2001, p. 3).

Differentiation Theory: An Experiential Approach

In a more experiential approach to differentiation, a brief exploration follows about how PLCs define, describe, discuss, and finally articulate their shared understanding of the concept of differentiated instruction. While it is important to read the literature and have the official, research-based descriptions in place, it is just as important to develop a shared definition that all teachers have embraced and can call their own. To that end, this section includes shared understandings or folksy sayings, analogies, metaphors, and brief glimpses of scenarios that help describe a differentiated classroom.

Differentiation to Practitioners

Definitions can be crafted from discussions and conversations within PLCs. An agreed-upon definition evolves from structured activities—such as brainstorms, comparisons, and classroom scenarios—that give all members a chance to articulate and explain their thinking, their prior knowledge, and their professional experiences. Then, from these talks, the teams arrive at real understandings of the concept that go far beyond the mere definition of terms and the recitation of research.

Sayings that attempt to define or characterize the differentiated instruction concept provide great conversation starters. Leaders let phrases such as the following percolate for a minute within the teams to set a context for the discussion on what differentiation is all about:

- Use different strokes for different folks.

- One size does not fit all.

- Differentiation does not mean louder and slower.

- Different is not necessarily differentiated.

- Change what needs changing.

- Differentiation is kids learning in their own time and in their own way.

Simple definitions evolve when teams try to wrap their minds around the idea of differentiation. Teams will often settle on a definition that may get tweaked many times along the way. Such definitions of differentiated instruction include:

- Differentiated instruction is student-centered, data-driven variation to a lesson.

- Differentiated instruction is differing the approach to learning for student needs.

- Differentiated instruction is doing whatever it takes to ensure students learn.

Brainstorming Synonyms

To help define differentiation, teams can brainstorm synonyms; the results may include words that don't appear in the more traditional written definitions. For example, if teachers in a professional learning session were asked to brainstorm words or phrases that come to mind when they think of differentiated instruction, and to let the connections happen spontaneously, they may come up with words such as *relevance, student needs, flexible, specialized, explicit, scaffold, purposeful, tiered, learning profile,* and *program.*

While *change, challenge,* and *choice* are words we readily associate with differentiated instruction, this brainstorm can yield additional and significant aspects of the concept of differentiation. More importantly, in the process of generating the word list, teachers in the PLC teams will engage in learning about differentiation from one another and will own the concept through the use of their own words.

Creating a Comparison

Another approach to defining the abstract concept of differentiation is comparing and contrasting it to concrete objects. Tools for describing differentiated instruction through comparison include direct comparisons, written analogies, and visual metaphors or pictures. The following feature box lists comparisons from PLC teams we have worked with as they searched for a common understanding of differentiation.

Differentiation is like a *garden*, because both take time to grow and grow at different rates; each has unique needs, and all represent a natural variety.

Differentiation is like a *school bus*, because both include everyone and pick up people where they are, and everyone arrives safely at their destinations.

Differentiation is like a *jungle*, because both have many ways to regenerate and reflect a diversity of the population, and there is a surprise at every turn.

Differentiation is like *clothes shopping*, because both show many options, there is something for everyone, and items can be altered if they don't fit.

Differentiation is like a *box of crayons*, because both have choice, create personal visions, and have pleasing results.

Differentiation is like a *snowflake*, because both are unique, distinctive, and multidimensional.

Differentiation is like a *diamond ring*, because both are multifaceted, no two the same, and each has a beauty of its own.

Differentiation is like an *octopus*, because both are adaptive, flexible, and reach out to others.

It is sometimes helpful to examine ideas when they are still works in progress; doing so gives a more developmental view of differentiation than the more formal discussion found in Tomlinson's work. In addition, some teams create accompanying visual aids to illustrate their comparisons.

Designing a Classroom Scenario

Finally, another method of defining and describing differentiated instruction is by designing a classroom scenario. For this activity, we asked each teacher in a PLC team to describe what a lesson in their classrooms might look like. In the following example, a differentiated seventh-grade math lesson was the focus:

> In my geometry class when we are working on the Pythagorean theorem and right triangles, I know how difficult it is for the kids to see how this idea is applied. I could differentiate by deliberately setting up the following three stations in my classroom with students rotating through during a block of time, thereby learning the content in three different ways:
>
> Station 1—Construction using right triangles
>
> Station 2—Drawing right triangles
>
> Station 3—Reading the text using a graphic organizer
>
> By the time the students have proceeded through the three stations, most of them will have it! For the one or two who don't, I will give them more direct help.

While this is a very short version of differentiating a lesson, it shows how teachers can manage this complex idea. Many teachers may not realize at first that they already differentiate to some degree. Understanding that it's not something new makes it easier for teachers to move forward in the PLC process of differentiated instruction.

Three Elements of Differentiated Learning

With both research-based and experience-based definitions in hand, it seems appropriate to summarize critical aspects of the differentiation concept before getting into the practical aspects of differentiating lessons and units. In this macroview, three principles emerge. While differentiation is complex and intricate, these three principles form the simple and elegant essence of differentiated instruction:

1 Change—content, process, product

2 Challenge—emotions, attention, memory

3 Choice—freedom within structure

First, we change something to make the learning more accessible to all learners; second, we challenge all learners at their level of understanding; and third, we allow students to have a level of choice in the teaching-learning process. All three elements should be intertwined to provide access to the lesson for every student.

Change

Differentiated instruction means changing something in the instructional process for the learner. Teachers must do something differently! Teaching differently is so much more than teaching the same thing louder and slower. Rather, it involves changing what students learn, how students learn it, and how students demonstrate what they have learned. Teaching differently means changing something substantive in the content, the process, or the product (Tomlinson, 1999a).

Changing the *content* implies that the teacher will change what the students are learning. Essentially, the teacher makes adjustments to the input by changing the complexity of the lesson, the resources used in the lesson, or in the learning environment. We discuss lesson complexity, resources, and environment more fully in chapter 4.

Changing the *process* involves offering alternative ways for students to learn. It means moving along a spectrum from teacher-directed instruction to more collaborative structures and student-directed inquiry. Chapter 5 focuses on direct instruction, cooperative learning, inquiry, and project learning, which make the lessons more accessible to students.

Changing the *products* of the lesson or the evidence of learning is about providing students with options in how they demonstrate their learning and the quality of that learning. Changes in the product mean offering multiple types of output that run the gamut from hands-on artifacts to authentic performances to traditional test results. Chapter 6 explores this differentiation element of student expression.

Challenge

Differentiated instruction means change, but change with appropriate challenge. Challenge engages the brain (Caine et al., 2009; Diamond & Hopson, 1998; Fogarty, 1997; Jensen, 2008; Sousa, 1995; Sylwester, 1995). Challenge also alerts the attention system in the brain by causing the student to attend to what is going on in the immediate environment. Because short-term memory precedes putting things into long-term memory and storing information for later retrieval (Sylwester, 1995), the importance of challenge in the classroom is quite significant.

Choice

Change and challenge must be combined with choice. Choice means opportunities for students to select the *what* and the *how* of the learning situation, but it doesn't mean complete freedom for students to decide everything about the teaching-learning process. It means freedom of choice within a given structure—for instance, choices about which of the three books they will read, or which of the twenty events they will attend for their reports. It means choices about how they will demonstrate their learning, based on an assortment of the eight multiple intelligences (Gardner, 1999): verbal/linguistic, visual/spatial, interpersonal/social, intrapersonal/self, mathematical/logical, musical/rhythmic, naturalist/physical world, and bodily/kinesthetic.

In brief, the teacher determines the structure, but builds in choice: choice with definite parameters that align with the expectations of the learning environment. It is generally accepted that students learn more when they feel they have some choice about the *what*, *when*, and *how*; when they have had some voice in the process; and when they feel ownership in the decision about their learning.

Within the framework of differentiation, the next task for PLC teams is to weave change, challenge, and choice into their instructional planning.

Using Data to Drive Differentiation

Data have a critical connection to the differentiation concept. Ongoing student data provide evidence of learning or gaps in the learning that help determine which instructional interventions students need. While we previously presented the brain science to support reasons why differentiation is needed, the data tell more specifically what kind of differentiation may be warranted.

Therefore, student achievement data are the catalyst for changing instruction in a PLC that supports differentiation. Student achievement data show teachers what is working and what is not, who is learning and who is not, and when a change in instruction is needed. Data tell the story of different learners and the need for different strategies, thereby illustrating the need for differentiated instruction.

For example, one way members of fully functioning PLCs support one another is by using relevant student data from many sources, including common assessments that they have developed, to make shared decisions. Following is a generic example of how a team of teachers working within the framework of a schoolwide PLC use data to drive instructional decisions after looking at the results of a common assessment. Table 2.1 shows the results of a common assessment for three fifth-grade classrooms on a fractions and decimals math unit. In this example, the test includes ten questions; the table breaks down the percentage of students by classroom who correctly answered each question.

Table 2.1: Sample Common Assessment Results: Percentage Correct

Question	Classroom A	Classroom B	Classroom C	Average
1	82%	80%	79%	80.3%
2	91%	79%	84%	84.6%
3	88%	77%	83%	82.6%
4	86%	81%	82%	83%
5	80%	81%	79%	80%
6	79%	61%	50%	63.3%
7	92%	52%	51%	65%
8	81%	79%	79%	79.6%
9	62%	52%	55%	56.3%
10	69%	48%	46%	54.3%

After looking at the data, the teachers conclude that the instructional goals in questions 6, 7, 9, and 10 were not met. The teachers also see that students in each of the three classrooms had problems, rather a single class bringing the average down for the whole grade-level team.

Before considering what they might do to reteach this content, teachers are best served by answering the question, "When did we teach this, and how did we teach it?" This simple question becomes a powerful reflective tool that focuses teachers on student results, because they understand that returning to their classrooms and teaching the content as they taught it the first time is not the wisest choice. They must examine what they did and how they can change it in order to differentiate the teaching.

These teachers also understand that differentiation doesn't mean that they individually design a separate lesson plan for every student. Differentiation means that teachers plan their teaching with robust, engaging instructional strategies that offer enough variety in content, process, and product to meet every student's needs. The goal of *Supporting Differentiated Instruction* is to help teacher teams use differentiation to guide specific interventions to reach every student and ensure student success. In brief, data drive this process.

Begin Slowly and Move Along

To ease into differentiated learning, teachers in learning communities may want to start slowly with low-preparation options and gradually move toward options that require more detailed preparation (Tomlinson, 2001).

Some of the "begin slowly" options include providing a choice of materials, focusing on using all levels of questioning, using more flexible seating arrangements, being mindful of the pacing and scaffolding of a lesson, and encouraging reading buddies and other kinds of cooperative learning structures.

To "move along" with differentiation strategies, teachers can do a number of things that require a little more preparation. These strategies include establishing learning centers in corners of the classroom and providing lessons with rotation stations that let students work on a skill or concept using several different modalities. Forming interest groups, choice boards, and multimodal product options are also effective measures. Finally, using problem-based learning and student contracts for independent investigations are powerful empowerment strategies for able students. The following feature box provides several strategies for both the begin-slowly and the move-along levels of instruction.

Begin Slowly	Move Along
Choice of materials	Learning centers
Reading buddies	Interest groups
Flexible seating	Rotation stations
Bloom's levels of questions	Choice boards
Pacing	Multimodal options
Scaffolding activities	Problem-based learning
	Student contracts

Action Options

This chapter explored the theory and practice of differentiation more deeply to set the stage for some preliminary work within PLC teams.

The Action Options for this chapter include a team activity called the Four-Fold Concept Development, in which the teams have an opportunity to dissect aspects of differentiation. In the second activity, the One-Minute Write, PLC members write personal reflections on aspects of changing instruction to meet student needs.

Action Option 1: Four-Fold Concept Development

After reading about differentiated learning, it is helpful to anchor the ideas with the Four-Fold Concept Development strategy. This activity allows team members to understand and explain their thoughts by making an abstract idea more concrete.

The Four-Fold Concept Development activity can be done in cooperative groups of four or fewer. The materials required include a large sheet of poster paper and magic markers. To begin the activity, one person in the group folds the paper in half and then in half again to create four equal sections (see fig. 2.1). Just before unfolding the paper, fold over the center corner of the paper so that when the paper is opened, there is a diamond shape in the middle of the four sections. Label the four sections *List*, *Rank*, *Compare*, and *Illustrate*, and write *Differentiation* in the center diamond (see fig. 2.1). (See page 43 for a reproducible of this activity. Visit **go.solution-tree .com/instruction** to download all reproducibles in this book.)

In this example, the team will unpack the term *differentiation*. First, using the List section of the paper, the groups take three minutes to brainstorm definitions, phrases, or synonyms that describe differentiation. The goal is at least twenty different words or phrases.

Second, the groups look over their lists and decide which three words or phrases best describe differentiation. These three top words go in the corner marked "Rank," and can be placed in ranking order. The ranking activity initiates a discussion of the ideas.

Third, teams compare differentiation to a concrete, tangible object or situation in the Compare corner. The team creates an analogy using the stem statement: "Differentiation is like _____, because both (1) _____, (2) _____ _____, and (3) _____." For instance, "Differentiation is like a multivitamin, because both (1) benefit everyone in different ways, (2) provide a healthy outcome, and (3) provide long-lasting, positive effects."

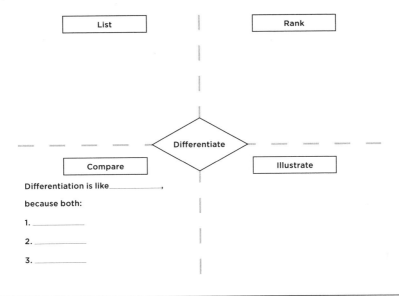

Figure 2.1: Sample four-fold concept development poster.

The final step in the Four-Fold Concept Development activity is to create a visual metaphor of the analogy in the Illustrate corner. In this example, the team draws a multivitamin and labels it with meaningful ideas, similar to a labeled diagram. This visual metaphor illuminates the analogy and the concept, and it lends another multimodal aspect to the activity.

Imagine the power of this activity for the classroom. It is a highly effective tool for unpacking difficult concepts, because it taps into many modalities and uses a collaborative approach to learning. The four steps can be managed over one class meeting or several.

Action Option 2: One-Minute Write

Here is a simple, highly engaging strategy that PLCs can use to focus on the issues of the day. It takes less than five minutes and is called the One-Minute Write (Stiggins, 2005).

Every member of the team participates, with one member serving as timekeeper. The goal is to focus on a single subject through writing. The One-Minute Write consists of two different writing sessions, each of which involves a specific, simple writing prompt, such as "change" (instead of "how change happens in schools"). A shorter prompt encourages divergent thinking resulting in more writing in the one-minute time period.

Give members a single sheet of paper each, a one-minute time limit, and instructions to write as much as they can, as fast as they can, using complete sentences. They should not take their pencils off the paper at any point. Once the prompt is given, the clock starts and the writing begins.

After the one-minute signal, ask members to count the total number of words and write that number on the paper. Then, ask them to circle—and count—the words with three or more syllables. Using these numbers as benchmarks, instruct team members to set a goal for the next one-minute write. They can try to write more total words, focusing on fluency, or they can try to write more three-syllable words, focusing on accuracy and precision of language. Both are skills of a good writer. Have them write their goals on their papers as well as tell their neighbors in order to publically commit to it.

Now, they are ready for the next writing exercise. The rules are the same as the first session, but the prompt is different. The second prompt should be similar to or complement the first. For example, instead of having teachers write about "change," which is the key concept of differentiated instruction, focus them on a complementary concept, such as "differentiation."

After the timekeeper calls the time for this second round, instruct participants to count the number of words, or syllables in words, to determine if they've reached their goals. Ask them to turn to a partner and discuss the strategy they used. Did they write in faster, shorter sentences or write in first person instead of second person? This conversation about their explicit strategy is the metacognitive reflection piece. Through these conversations, participants have a chance to reflect on their thought processes and share their thinking with one another, while simultaneously unpacking the partner concepts of change and differentiation.

In essence, the One-Minute Write acts as a mini-assessment of individual members' understanding of the concepts in question, while also addressing writing strategies. This assessment sets the stage with the *what* question and leads to the *how*. It also allows teachers to model the standard writing behaviors they want students to mirror in their classrooms. For example, in a lesson about the food chain, a teacher may have students write about *plants* with the follow-up *insects*.

Four-Fold Concept Development Activity

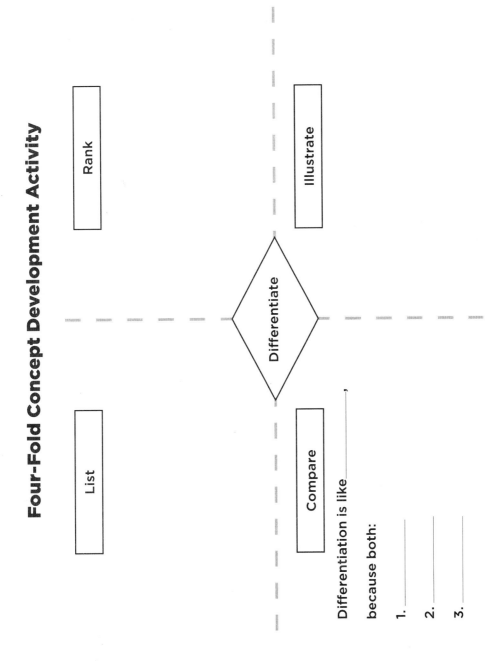

Rank

Illustrate

List

Compare

Differentiate

Differentiation is like _____,

because both:

1. _____

2. _____

3. _____

CHAPTER 3

ALL ABOUT THE LEARNERS

PLC TAKE AWAY

Learning How Student Data Support Differentiation

This chapter explains the need for initial student data that identify who the learners are and what their talents and needs are—their "backstories." Teachers need to know what makes their learners tick. This chapter focuses on understanding learners and accommodating their learning styles in ways that allow them to excel.

When teachers deliberately and purposefully seek baseline data on their students, they give themselves a huge advantage. When there are reasons to differentiate, teachers inform their decisions on accommodating, adjusting, and modifying a lesson for particular students with whatever information they have about those students. That is what the differentiation process is all about. The data come in many forms, including face-to-face interactions, anecdotal classroom records, standardized test data, and the common assessments used to monitor student progress.

To proceed with this critical aspect of the differentiated classroom, PLC teams should use various tools and techniques to assess their students in four specific areas: (1) student readiness, (2) student interests, (3) student learning profiles, and (4) student affect (Tomlinson, 2005). Student readiness is directly linked to potential for immediate and future growth, while student interests spark the motivation to learn. Learning profiles that delineate preferred styles and learning strengths and weaknesses impact the efficiency of student learning, while student affect speaks to the feelings, emotions, and attitudes of the learners.

> Student readiness—ability and effort; what is challenging and attainable?
>
> Student interests—hobbies and pastimes; what evokes curiosity and passion?
>
> Student learning profiles—strengths and weaknesses; what supports their learning?
>
> Student affect—feelings and attitudes; what is the gateway to success?
>
> *Source: Tomlinson, 2001*

Student Readiness

In any attempt to assess students, their readiness to learn is a primary factor. Tomlinson (2001) often refers to readiness in terms of knowledge and skills in a related area of learning. Assessing student readiness involves appraising students' abilities, their knowledge bases, and the depth and breadth of that knowledge. It requires the evidence of understanding that accompanies achievement as well as evidence of the intensity of effort. Knowing about students' abilities and being aware of their readiness to learn new information helps teachers determine what might be challenging and what will be attainable.

Learning is grounded in students' prior knowledge and background experiences. It is important to ask what students know, what books they have read, and what experiences they have had. For teachers to make good decisions about what they want students to know, they need a starting point. They need to know what materials to use to guarantee that students will grasp what is being taught, and they need to know how to determine if students have learned what they set out to learn. And, finally, revisiting the final essential question, teachers need to know what they will do when students have or haven't learned. This process begins and ends with deep knowledge of the students.

Achievement Levels

Achievement levels are evident from standardized test scores and achievement data readily available in the schools. In fact, student results, class results, and school results are the bread-and-butter data that learning communities rely on as they analyze and discuss the students in their classes. PLCs are privy to an abundance of information generated from these sophisticated testing systems that produce disaggregated data, graphed reports, analytical charts, numerous comparisons, and rigorous recommendations. Part of the PLC mission is to utilize data to help determine learning paths for students.

In addition to the all-important data generated from the testing system, teacher teams also have student grades, grade point averages, reports, and report card data to use in their assessment of students' readiness levels. Grades, rankings, and teacher-generated reports provide a long-term perspective of the students' achievements and readiness to learn, even though this information appears to be more subjective than test data.

Knowledge Bases

Students' knowledge bases are also a helpful indicator of ability and readiness. Reports and school records provide clues as to the actual subject matter content to which students have been exposed, including listings of courses taken, grades completed, and a general profile of the knowledge base that students have to build upon. PLCs committed to obtaining as much baseline data as possible about each student find all these measures valuable in creating student profiles.

Intellect

Student intellect is another measure of readiness levels. While teachers used to have data on every student from group IQ tests that were administered to the entire student body, schools no longer use these measures as a general screening device. The results of these kinds of intelligence tests are controversial at best, and often debunked as too narrow in their scope, inaccurate in their assessments, and overvalued in their ability to project future success. However, when results designate students for more intense screening, individual tests of general intellectual abilities are sometimes used as a further measure. They are, in essence, given to help prescribe learning plans for and diagnose selected students who have learning difficulties or who may exhibit rare talents and intellectual giftedness. When this type of information is available, teachers can examine it for tips on how to approach a student's learning style. When it is not available, teachers may request it if it seems pertinent to their baseline data for a particular student.

Level of Effort

Finally, in the search for relevant information about student readiness levels, teachers can pay attention to a student's level of effort. Effort is considered the "other side of the report card" by teachers, yet often it does not carry the same weight as grades. In *Classroom Instruction That Works*, Marzano, Pickering, and Pollock (2001) examine the strategy of reinforcing effort as a best practice in instruction and its power in determining success. Effort reigns over other elements included in the success formula, such as natural ability, luck, and knowing someone who can expedite the situation. Effort is huge in the overall success of students in school, as well as in life endeavors. Thus, PLC teams are wise to include discussions about student effort as they develop their understandings of student readiness levels.

In summary, readiness levels are composed of what students know, what they understand, and what they are able to do. Learning is constructed in the mind of the learner. That constructed meaning depends on the scaffolding of prior knowledge and past experience. The more teachers know about the scaffolding that is already in place for each student, the more skillful they can be in their planning and execution of the next steps in the construction process.

Student Interests

Student interests are the second concern teachers examine as they try to get to know their students. Again, to cite the authority, Tomlinson (2003) describes interests as those pursuits that evoke curiosity and passion in a learner. Thus, highly effective teacher teams working within PLCs attend both to existing interests and developing undiscovered interests in their students. By finding out about their students in more personal ways—by identifying their interests and their passions—teachers obtain powerful motivational tools to ignite student learning. In many cases, it is through a particular, known interest that teachers find keys to students' learning paths.

The spectrum of student interests that teachers can explore includes everything from hobbies to sports. Although it is somewhat difficult to learn everything about every kid, especially at the high school level where the numbers of students are so large, it serves PLC teams well to learn as much as possible about each and every student they serve. Such knowledge—students' likes and dislikes in movies, music, media, and even the kinds of foods they prefer—proves invaluable.

It is also important to recognize when students show genuine curiosity about something that interests them and when they have a real passion for something that has hooked them. These kinds of experiences create the real connections between the teacher and the student. When PLC teams make a deliberate effort to get to know their students well, they create relational ties with students that lead to respect and trust.

Teachers in PLC teams have many means to find out what makes a student unique, what motivates him or her, and what measures will be necessary to move that student on to the next step in his or her education. These methods include interest inventories, student journals and portfolios, advisement time, and informal conversations with students directly or indirectly.

Interest Inventories

Interest inventories can be as simple as having students complete their own interest cards, which ask students to provide three to five personal preferences such as favorite sport, book, movie, food, and nickname; or they can be more comprehensive, such as published interest inventories that yield a comprehensive listing ranging from pastimes to preferences for activities both in school and out of school. These inventories are available online for various grade levels, and can be very helpful in generating a clear profile of a student's likes and dislikes.

Student Journals

Student journals are also common introspective tools used in the classroom. Teachers often use journaling as a reflective tool for students to record their thoughts, concerns, and triumphs in the school setting and even in their personal lives. The journals are private, and when shared with teachers, they are treated with trust and confidentiality. The journals are introspective tools and, as such, must be handled by students and teachers with care and respect.

Advisement Time

Advisement time—a scheduled period during the week—is a strategy that promotes insight into student interests and motivation. This strategy originated with middle schools and now has been adopted by some high schools, particularly for freshmen. This dedicated time offers opportunities for personal advisement to a small, reasonable number of students, who meet with a caring adult to discuss and debrief on pressing concerns and urgent needs. Usually, this group meets all year long; relationships build, rapport develops, and a climate of trust and caring prevails. In response to success stories of this model, some schools are beginning to structure advisement time as a four-year commitment to the same groups of students with the same advisor. Information garnered in these advisory sessions can be shared, confidentially, with the PLC team to provide further data on students in need.

Informal Conversations

While advisement time is a specific structure used to promote conversations with students, many informal conversations and various other activities help PLCs learn about students as well. When teachers attend school events, sponsor school clubs, coach sports, and participate in different ways in the extracurricular activities, they have prime time to get to their students from entirely different perspectives.

When teachers in PLC teams become aware of students in this holistic way, when they see them in formal classroom interactions as well as in more informal situations, they learn more about students' likes and dislikes, sports interests, and hobbies. These kinds of subjects help teachers understand student motivation. The saying "They don't care what you know until they know you care" spells out the true value in getting to know what turns particular students onto learning. PLC teams pursue this end by getting to know students continuously and consistently in as many ways as possible.

Student Learning Profiles

A third target of baseline data is students' personal learning profiles. Tomlinson (2005), the leading voice in this area of differentiation, often talks about learning profiles as ways of determining how students learn best. These include gender, culture, learning style, and intelligence preference. If classrooms can offer and support different modes of learning, it is likely that more students will learn effectively and efficiently.

Teachers should consider gender factors and cultural needs first in their individual student inventories. In these two critical areas, PLC teams are wise to educate themselves as an ongoing part of their PLC work. This chapter's Action Options (page 56) include specific resources. Other areas of concern, as teachers turn their attention to gathering learner profile information, include looking at learning-style preferences and creating multiple intelligences profiles. To collect and consider this information, teachers use methods and measures that include published or teacher-made surveys of preferred learning styles and inventories of multiple intelligences profiles. Visit http://surfaquarium.com/MI/inventory.htm for one such inventory. By knowing the learners' profiles, teachers can tap into those areas of strength and tailor the instruction for more efficient learning and positive results.

A closer look at the kinds of information-gathering techniques used frequently by the PLC teams in their personal surveys of students follows.

Gender Factors

Gender factors include such topics as classroom bullying, mean girls, and the rising failure and dropout rates of males. There is ongoing controversy about single-sex schools and single-sex classes, and the benefits and detriments of both. Gender is one area of study PLC teams will want to consider as they disaggregate their student achievement data and review the findings. If gender issues arise, a book study with discussion questions and structured debriefings about the implications for the students and the school might be helpful. It is yet another way of getting to know more about the students.

Cultural Background

In addressing cultural background and related issues, again, many rich resources are available to PLC teams. A powerful strategy is to invite guest speakers, representative of the various cultures integral to the school demographics, to talk with the learning communities. These kinds of interactions extend the professional conversations of the team beyond the norm. They inform the uninformed in genuinely visceral ways and the impact stretches back to the kids and the cultures they embrace. In the end, these kinds of interactions with the community create authentic connections between the school and the community itself.

Learning Styles

Learning styles or learning preferences (Dunn & Dunn, 1998; Gregorc, 1982; Myers, 1962) represent another area of self-awareness for students, and they provide teachers with knowledge about students. Teachers hear students say things like, "I'm such a visual learner. I have to see it to really understand it," "I'm just not very creative," "I'm into music. That's something I can really get into. If I put these words to music, I can remember the whole thing the first time through," or "I am really a concrete thinker. I like to get my hands on an idea in a tangible way. I need to put it together, to build a model to understand it." This type of comment cues teachers on how to best approach certain learners. Teachers can file away these facts as they get to know their crew of kids and as they think about how to reach them and teach them.

Learning-style inventories often use either/or terminology such as *concrete* or *abstract*, *sequential* or *random*, *willing* or *reticent*, *able* or *unable*, *motivated* or *reluctant*. To incorporate a learning styles inventory into classroom work, consult the resources listed in the Action Options (page 56). Teachers can easily administer these inventories, which make great socialization icebreakers as teachers get to know or reacquaint themselves with students.

In brief, the idea of learning styles is related to the idea of learning modalities. In their most simple form, modalities are often summarized in three succinct categories: visual, auditory, and kinesthetic. Visual learners tend to use phrases such as, "I see . . ." or "Do you see what I mean?" (Costa & Garmston, 2002). They prefer visual stimuli and respond to graphic organizers, maps, and charts. Auditory learners tend to get more from lecture formats, may read aloud to themselves, and learn well through conversing, hearing, and processing information. Kinesthetic learners are hands-on and prefer concrete, tangible ways of learning new information. All three modalities working in concert provide the most robust learning opportunities.

Intelligences

Two theories of intelligence offer alternatives to the usual idea of a single, general intelligence. These theories pluralize *intelligence* into multiple forms. While these theories are sometimes questioned quite rigorously, they serve the educational community in their effort to help teachers understand the various aspects of the learners.

The first theory, espoused by Howard Gardner (1999), is called the theory of multiple intelligences. The second is the triarchic theory of intelligence, shaped by Robert Sternberg's work (1988). This discussion looks briefly at both theories, because they provide keys to tapping into student potentials to learn efficiently and effectively.

Theory of Multiple Intelligences

Gardner's theory (1999) puts forth the idea that each individual exhibits a profile of intelligences in differing amounts and strengths. Drawing on his research of prodigies in the field, each of whom strongly exhibits a certain intelligence, Gardner's theory describes eight identified intelligences: verbal/linguistic, visual/spatial, interpersonal/social, intrapersonal/self, mathematical/logical, musical rhythmic, naturalist/physical world, and bodily/kinesthetic. We've listed these eight intelligences or talents in the following feature box with a sampling of people who have that particular intelligence in abundance.

> Verbal/linguistic intelligence—William Shakespeare, Emily Dickinson, Walt Whitman
>
> Visual/spatial intelligence—Claude Monet, Pablo Picasso, Georgia O'Keeffe
>
> Interpersonal/social intelligence—Dale Carnegie, Oprah Winfrey, Barack Obama
>
> Intrapersonal/self intelligence—Mother Teresa, Mahatma Gandhi, the Dalai Lama
>
> Mathematical/logical intelligence—Albert Einstein, Archimedes, Bill Gates
>
> Musical/rhythmic intelligence—Wolfgang Amadeus Mozart, Ludwig van Beethoven, Itzhak Perlman
>
> Naturalist/physical world intelligence—Charles Darwin, John James Audubon, Jane Goodall
>
> Bodily/kinesthetic intelligence—Hercules, Arthur Ashe, Tiger Woods

We define the different intelligences briefly here in text, and expand them with classroom examples in the Action Options (page 56) at the end of the chapter.

The *verbal/linguistic intelligence* sets humans apart from other species. Oral and written language allows humans to communicate in sophisticated ways. It is the honored intelligence in school and reigns supreme in its impact on the student success in K–12 classrooms. It is the intelligence of trial lawyers, authors, and statesmen.

The *visual/spatial intelligence* is captured in the visual arts of painting, drawing, drafting, and the like. It is the intelligence of the artist. The visual/spatial intelligence imprints learning on the brain in the form of images, graphics, and indelible pictures that are retrieved consciously and subconsciously in one's memory system.

The *interpersonal/social intelligence* is in the affective domain, and it governs sociability and relationship building. This is the intelligence of skillful salesmen, pastors, and counselors. It is the intelligence that propels communication, trust building, and conflict resolution.

On the other hand, the *intrapersonal/self intelligence* is the potential to know one's self. It is the introspective intelligence of self-awareness, self-assessment, and self-knowledge that allows people to grow and develop as self-fulfilled human beings. This is the intelligence of philosophers and poets, prophets and shamans.

The *mathematical/logical intelligence* is that of abstract reasoning, mathematical thinking, and scientific hypotheses and proofs. It is the intelligence that draws logical conclusions and makes reasoned inferences about the natural and abstract laws of physics, math, and science as well as the logic of thinking in any and every discipline. This intelligence is at work in the complicated calculations of the calculus classroom and in the sequence of an intricate plot in a novel.

The *musical/rhythmic intelligence* is expressed through music appreciation as well as musical ability and performance. It is the intelligence of vocalists, instrumentalists, and symphonic conductors. This is the intelligence of a highly acute auditory intelligence that hears things differently. Individuals with this intelligence are connoisseurs of sound.

Added by Gardner, in 1998, to the original seven intelligences, the *naturalist/physical world intelligence* refers to the world of flora and fauna and hierarchical thinking. In turn, Gardner considers this the intelligence of the natural environment in which one lives, whether it be an African jungle or a concrete jungle. It is the intelligence of geologists and botanists, gardeners, and astronomers.

Finally, the *bodily/kinesthetic intelligence* is that of the athlete, dancer, and sculptor. It is also the intelligence of the chef, carpenter, and massage therapist. This is the intelligence that learns by doing and literally uses the hands to assimilate the essence of the concept through a project or performance.

Gardner goes on to say that it behooves school personnel to design learning in ways that tap into and exercise each of the eight intelligences in a balanced curricular setting. He believes that a robust and richly varied approach to instruction allows students many entry points into the learning and many expressive modes to demonstrate what they know and are able to do.

Without overstating the import of this theory, it captures the essence of differentiation in broad brushstrokes that some PLC teams manage quite easily. Others, however, are not as sure what this theory looks like in terms of delivery of standards-based classroom content. This is where the PLC teams come in. Multiple intelligences are key to diverse instructional strategies, and these ideas often need some unpacking for true implementation in classrooms. PLC teams must address multimodal learning when they explore differentiation as a practical teaching technique.

Triarchic Theory of Intelligence

In the second theory, the triarchic theory of intelligence, Sternberg proposes three intelligences: analytical, creative, and practical. We have suggested some well-known names associated with each of these categories in the following feature box.

Analytical intelligence—Socrates, Bill Gates, Stephen Hawking, Marie Curie

Creative intelligence—Maria Tallchief, Alfred Hitchcock, Pablo Picasso, Frank Lloyd Wright

Practical intelligence—Albert Einstein, Oprah Winfrey, Steve Jobs, Larry Page, Sergey Brin

The *analytical intelligence* is described as linear, sequential thinking that is synonymous with critical thinking skills such as evaluation, justification, and classification. The analytical intelligence is the most valued in school. This intelligence is sometimes referred to as "schoolhouse smart" because people in this category are excellent at explaining, outlining, diagramming, and prioritizing.

The *creative intelligence* is that of the innovator, inventor, and artist. This intelligence sees the world and looks for ways to change and improve it. Creative intelligence thinks outside the box and asks what-if questions. This is the intelligence of the entrepreneur because its strong suits include generating, producing, showing, improving, and connecting.

The *practical intelligence* is that of the pragmatist because it is contextual by nature. It is to the point, results oriented, and focused on the bottom line. This intelligence utilizes the context of the situation and searches for relevant solutions. The focus is on application and usefulness. This is the intelligence often referred to as "street smart" because members in this category demonstrate, show, develop, and solve.

Again, the examination of these intelligences often yields great conversations within PLC teams as they get to know their students. When teachers understand and utilize these intelligences in the classroom, they are better able to provide students with personalized doorways to learning.

Student Affect

The fourth and final area of baseline assessment that yields valuable information about various students is student affect. Tomlinson (2005) defines student affect as how students feel about themselves, their work, and the classroom as a whole. She sees it as a gateway to helping each student become more fully engaged and successful in learning.

As teachers explore this very human component of individual students, they become aware of student attitudes, dispositions, Habits of Mind, issues of self-concept, and evidence of self-esteem levels.

Attitudes are about the motivational postures students assume; "I can! I will! I did!" is a different attitudinal posture than "I can't! I won't! I didn't!" Teachers must be aware of the attitudes projected by students and differentiate accordingly to find the particular keys to learning for each student.

Dispositions are similar to attitudes, but for the sake of this discussion, dispositions are treated as broader brushstrokes. One might describe a student as having a sunny disposition, reticent manner, or caring demeanor. Dispositions seem to define what might be called "the sense of presence" when one is around that student. They are emotional postures students assume.

The *Habits of Mind*, as presented by Costa and Kallick (2009), include a set of sixteen character traits, among which are creating, persisting, risking, wonderment, accuracy, flexibility, questioning, and tolerance for ambiguity. These Habits of Mind speak volumes about students and their pathways to success. They are yet another source of information for PLC teams.

Self-concept is captured in the adage "I'm okay, you're okay," (Harris, 2004) in which students express their sense of self, or how they see and define themselves. They may say things like, "I'm a good student," "I see myself as a loyal friend," or "I am always the one in my family to try to make peace and keep things harmonious." These students have insight into themselves.

Self-esteem, on the other hand, is how students feel about themselves—how confident or tentative they believe themselves to be, how positively or negatively they feel about themselves, their hair, their bodies, their intellects, their reading abilities, and so on. Do they feel good or bad about themselves? Do they feel joyfully competent or woefully inadequate? Do they feel successful or lacking?

All of these student affects are important pieces to the puzzle of learning for each and every student serviced by the PLC. Awareness of these character traits provides insights and ideas for working with students and facilitating their success.

Inventory Options

This chapter focuses on the types of data that provide a comprehensive, multifaceted picture of students. It explains why all kinds of baseline data are helpful in getting to know the students and why this kind of in-depth information allows teachers to better facilitate successful school experiences and achievement results for all students.

In closing, the following feature box provides a quick look at various student inventories that complete student profiles. These include links about gender, cultural background, multiple intelligences, learning styles, and student interests and motivation. Visit **go.solution-tree.com/instruction** for live versions of all links mentioned in this book.

Multiple Intelligences Inventory

- Simple multiple intelligences inventory—http://homepages.wmich.edu/
  ~buckleye/miinventory.htm
- In-depth multiple intelligences inventory—http://surfaquarium.com/MI/
  inventory.htm

Learning Styles Inventory

- Finding strengths—www.ldrc.ca/projects/miinventory/mitest.html
- Learning styles online—www.learning-styles-online.com/inventory
- Learning styles inventory—www.personal.psu.edu/bxb11/LSI/LSI.htm

Analytical, Creative, Practical Intelligences

- Triarchic theory inventory—www.schultzcenter.org/pdf/sternberg
  _inventory.pdf
- Learning style self-assessment—www.ldpride.net/learning-style-test.html

---

Action Options

PLC TAKE AWAY

Learning How Student Data Support Differentiation

When giving someone directions, the first thing we say is, "Where are you?" Why do we ask that question? Because the most detailed, well-worded directions are irrelevant if we don't know where we are starting. Just as travelers review maps before the trip begins, teachers assess before they teach. The assessment may be as simple as, "How many have heard of the state of Hawaii?" The response determines the teacher's next steps.

When differentiating instruction, it is essential that PLC teams not only understand how to differentiate, but also why. Baseline data provide PLC teams with the initial data they need to understand what worked and didn't work in the past, why it worked or didn't work, and how they might differentiate for various students. Through the reflective, collegial dialogues at the heart of learning communities, teachers determine the talents and needs of their students. In this way, they are better able to differentiate instruction for the student body they serve.

The Action Options that follow examine the concepts in this chapter more thoroughly with several activities for PLC teams to use in their efforts toward student success. These tools help identify students' traits, talents, and learning profiles. These student self-assessment tools create a picture of the whole student, including strengths and weaknesses. By using these kinds of appraisal tools, students and teachers often gain understanding and insights that greatly impact student learning and success. Visit www.allthingsplc.info/wordpress/?m=200907 for more information on managing assessment data.

Action Option 1: Identifying Student Traits

PLCs are effective when they keep the focus on the students. Identifying a particular student's traits helps members of PLCs see possible entryways into that student's learning potentials.

To do this particular activity, each member takes a single sheet of paper and folds it horizontally into thirds, like a letter. This creates a type of trifold brochure. On the front, title the brochure "Identifying Student Traits." On the inside left panel, write "Student Readiness," "Student Interests," and "Student Learning Profile" in a column. On the inside right panel, write "What?," "How?," and "Why?" headings in a column (see fig. 3.1, page 58). (See page 60 for a reproducible of this activity. Visit **go.solution-tree.com/instruction** to download all reproducibles in this book.)

Each member of the learning community selects a different student of concern, who can be a past or current student. The teacher then writes that student's name at the top of the brochure's center section and draws a picture of the student. The drawing forces the teacher to mentally picture the student and to foster thinking about the student.

Teachers then identify the student's traits using the three headings in the left panel. They write shorthand notes as they think about the student. Next, the teachers address the questions on the right panel: What do they differentiate with this student? How do they differentiate? Why do they differentiate? The *why* is particularly important. Articulating the reasons they make individual instructional decisions about a specific student is a powerful exercise.

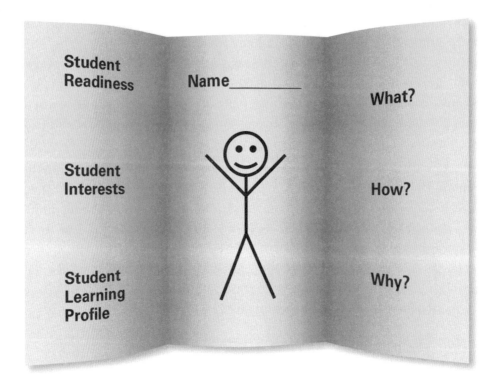

Figure 3.1: Sample student-traits brochure.

After completing the ideas for differentiation, the members of the PLC team share, in pairs, about the students they each selected to study. Taking time to remember and talk about specific students of concern emphasizes that differentiation is about what teachers do to connect to the individuals in their classes. This reflective dialogue lays the groundwork for future conversations about what's working and what's not working with particular students.

This same activity can be used with a single student as the focus for everyone; members identify traits from their perspectives of this student. Each teacher on the team interacts with students in different ways from different vantage points, depending on what he or she teaches and how the student responds to that subject and teacher. This total team focus on one student has amazing potential to reveal the many aspects of a student that impact his or her learning. It is a powerful strategy to use when a student is in trouble, but also a viable tool for students who are quiet, soft spoken, or never the center of attention. This may be the intense focus needed for the PLC to know this child in a different way.

In summary, this deliberate focus on one student is likened to candling an egg. *Candling* means examining the egg by holding it to light, making the inside visible. This close examination of a student, from all angles and from every perspective, provides a transparency for knowing that student intently and in a different way than before.

Activity Option 2: "It's All About Me" Cards

Using a 5 × 9-inch index card, have students within the PLC group complete "It's All About Me" cards to identify five attributes about themselves. They place their comments in the four corners and the center by category: top right, significant personality trait; top left, favorite pastime; bottom right, favorite quote; bottom left, special talent; and center, name and sibling order (see fig. 3.2). These cards can become catalysts for interaction with the students, turned in for PLC teams to scrutinize, or used as a conferencing tool with teachers and students. (See page 61 for a reproducible of this activity. Visit **go.solution-tree.com/instruction** to download all reproducibles in this book.)

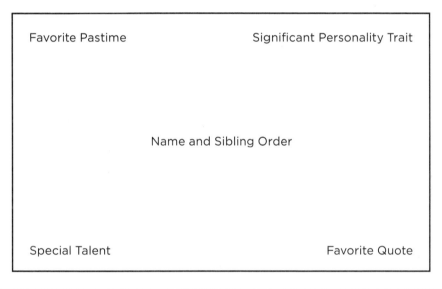

Figure 3.2: Sample "It's all about me" card for the classroom.

Identifying Student Traits Brochure

What?

How?

Why?

Name _____

Student Readiness

Student Interests

Student Learning Profile

"It's All About Me" Cards

Favorite Pastime   Significant Personality Trait

Name and Sibling Order

Special Talent   Favorite Quote

- - - - - - - - - - - - - - - - - - - -

Favorite Pastime   Significant Personality Trait

Name and Sibling Order

Special Talent   Favorite Quote

CHAPTER 4

CHANGING THE CONTENT

PLC TAKE AWAY

Learning How Teachers Differentiate Content to Meet Student Needs

Changing the content is the first of three areas (content, process, and product) that professional learning communities focus on as they delve into supporting differentiated instruction. This chapter centers on the methods and means PLC teams use as they focus specifically on how to change the content for students in order to make learning more accessible. In particular, it analyzes the relationship between differentiating instruction and the standards of learning teachers are accountable to teach.

PLC teams must make critical decisions in their ongoing curriculum work. They must determine what standards-based content to teach as they answer the essential question: what do we want students to know? Then, and only then, does the discussion turn to how teachers might change the content in explicit ways to differentiate for certain learner needs. The focus is on changing the agreed-upon content to enable student access to the information without changing the standard. This chapter first explains the boundaries of content differentiation and then provides examples for three places teachers can change the content: (1) the complexity of the lesson, (2) the resources within the lesson, and (3) the environment or context of the lesson. We provide in-depth examples for elementary, middle, and high school situations.

These techniques are core ideas that PLCs use to understand the mechanics of supporting differentiated instruction by changing the content to be more accessible to students. But first we must address the issue of standards-based curriculum and what teams can and cannot change in the curriculum.

Content Standards

The first and most fundamental issue that emerges in PLC team discussions is the concept of content standards. The dual requirements of maintaining the required student learning standards and simultaneously changing the content to meet student needs seems contradictory at first glance.

Standards of learning speak to the curriculum content that is delineated for teachers and learners. Subject matter content, outlined in the standards, sets expectations for exactly what students should know and be able to do. Typically, the content standards include facts, data, concepts, skills, attitudes, dispositions, principles, and Habits of Mind in particular discipline areas. In addition, standards often delineate life skills such as problem solving, teamwork, and communication. The early work of the learning community often involves a confirmation of the critical power standards—the content they want students to learn in the various disciplines.

Differentiated learning speaks to the methods by which that learning occurs, to the diversity of the learners, and to the many approaches to learning for those learners. Differentiation is the process of finding appropriate entry points (Gardner, 1999) into learning and appropriate exit points for expressing the learning. It's about changing something in the teaching-learning process and having a repertoire of teaching strategies for various situations.

There must be many ways for students to learn and to demonstrate their learning of a standard. When these two concepts—standards of learning and differentiated instruction—work together, students become the focus of schooling. They are exposed to a standard curriculum that sets high expectations for all, and—at the same time—they are allowed to learn content in personally relevant ways. Both the teaching and learning processes are fully honored: the standards honor the accepted curriculum teachers are required to teach and are held accountable for, and differentiated learning honors the full range of diverse learners found in most classrooms. The discussion that follows reveals how to simultaneously respect standards and differentiate the content.

As mentioned previously, we've divided content change into three categories: (1) changing the complexity or sophistication of the content by making the material concrete, symbolic, or abstract; (2) changing the resources within the lesson with informational, narrative, multimedia, and human interactions; and (3) changing the environment or context of the lesson by using the classroom, the school building, the neighborhood, the community, or a virtual classroom. Each of these powerful and diverse measures is elaborated on in the following discussion, with comprehensive explanations and examples.

Changing the Complexity

Effective teachers do this strategy already. They change the activity to provide a rich, diverse, multimodal approach for the entire class. They know how to provide those differing entry points for the learners, and they offer various perspectives to help students achieve a deep understanding. Effective teachers not only use a variety of instructional activities with the whole class, but they use these same differentiated approaches with small groups or with individual students, when necessary, to accommodate learning. In essence, these teachers already differentiate by changing the content by using appropriate resources for different students.

It is not uncommon to observe teachers using several approaches to teach a new concept. While teachers are already accommodating learners with the sophistication level of the content, they may not label it as a differentiated learning approach. That is where PLC teams come in.

Learning communities share a range of creative activities and proven strategies from their teaching repertoires, taking the lesson through various stages of complexity. They share concrete activities to make it hands-on, visual tools to make it visibly understandable, and strategies to make abstract ideas comprehensible and clear to learners. In effect, PLC teams collaborate on explicit, meaningful differentiation of complexity levels, with student success clearly in mind.

A robust example of changing content is the tiered lesson. Tiered lessons are strategic and useful lesson-planning tools. Teachers use three tiers of learning to change the complexity of the content and provide various levels of challenge and appropriate student choices. The most basic level of complexity is the *concrete level*, in which students use objects to learn. The next tier of content complexity is the *symbolic level*, in which the content is represented in pictures or illustrations. The third tier is the *abstract level*, in which words and ideas convey a learning experience. Teachers with rich repertoires know how to orchestrate all three tiers to challenge students.

Concrete Tier

Elementary classroom learning centers epitomize the concrete levels of learning: writing centers, listening centers, science centers, and reading corners. In middle and high school, concrete hands-on learning occurs unabashed in the form of programs such as integrated technology, automotive shop, vocational, and consumer arts.

Concrete learning levels abound in experimentation and investigations of all kinds. Any activity that involves manipulation, construction, or building—models, prototypes, demonstration sites, and the like—is a marvelous example of how teachers offer this most basic, most foundational level of hands-on learning.

Symbolic Tier

This tier is all about *seeing* how things work. The symbolic level of activities includes the use of drawings, sketches, diagrams, cartoons, and even comics. Symbolic activities represent ideas through a plethora of graphic organizers: concept and mind maps, attribute webs, Venn diagrams, flowcharts, fishbone analyses charts, thought trees, cause-and-effect circles, and teacher- and student-made graphic tools. Hyerle's (2009) thinking maps provide a grand resource of these representational tools.

This tier includes visual renderings and images, including film and online media such as YouTube, TeacherTube, and Hulu. It delivers content through symbols and symbolic language, just as international signage does, for example, by representing *no* with a circle divided by a diagonal line. This type of representation presents content in ways that allow learners to literally see the ideas.

Abstract Tier

It's important to recognize that teachers use the abstract level, the most sophisticated level of instruction, most often. Common abstract teaching techniques include textbook readings and lectures. While teachers may vary the textbook assignments by resources and requirements or vary the lectures by length and duration, they should recognize that while some students learn readily through these more abstract methods of sharing content, others don't.

Using the Tiers

A lesson on magnets illustrates an elementary example of designing learning opportunities for the three tiers. At the concrete level, the students work with magnets and objects in a hands-on investigation. At the symbolic level, students view a video about magnets and then draw scientific diagrams depicting the direction of the magnetic fields in various instances. At the abstract level, informative lectures by an expert complement textbook readings, and students discuss the sophisticated concept of magnetic pull. While the content is similar, the delivery of that content in each tier is quite diverse.

In a middle to high school example, teachers may set up three learning stations in a block-schedule class, each of which uses one of the three tiers of complexity. Students rotate around the three stations during class, experiencing the learning in different ways. Or the teacher may actually use all three tiers in a series of three class periods, allowing students longer exposure to the various methods of learning the content. The teacher could also simply scaffold all three tiers for the whole class when complex concepts are introduced.

It is important to remember that change is only one of the three principles of differentiation, along with challenge and choice. To build in the elements of challenge and choice, the teacher can ask students to select the station that appeals to their learning styles or that is the most challenging for them. Over time, students recognize how they learn best. Whenever possible, teachers should set the parameters for powerful learning options.

To gain more ideas, teachers can share familiar methods for changing content in their collaborative conversations as PLC teams. For instance, perhaps they discuss the use of shared lectures in which students prepare and deliver some parts of the content as guest speakers, or they share other materials and information sources that might suit a certain student's ability levels.

As PLC teams discuss and debrief on the many ways to differentiate the complexity of the content, they will see the power of collegial sharing and the opportunities it offers to improve and increase their repertoire of teaching strategies. These exciting conversations epitomize, in very practical ways, how PLC teams support differentiated instruction.

At the end of this chapter (page 73), you'll find more elementary, middle, and high school examples of changing the complexity or sophistication of the content.

Changing the Resources

Varying the kinds of resources and the complexity of those resources offers a familiar content differentiation option used frequently by quality teachers. Many schools have depositories for old and used materials in which teachers can find optional or supplemental resources. Resources can also be found in the library, the media center, or on appropriate, credible websites. Staff can confer about assembling a bank of resources for an upcoming unit as well. Quality teachers in PLC teams know that using and sharing many sources brings differentiated instruction to life.

Changing resources is an invaluable tool. It opens many doorways for students by letting them find the resource that is right for them—the book, the article, the medium, or the person. Changing resources simply means tailoring the type and level of information for student accessibility.

Type of Information

Teachers must be aware of the various types of information available to best reach each student. Publishers of textbooks and student materials may take different approaches to learning. At the elementary to middle school levels, for example, some science texts are heavily illustrated, whereas others are dense with text and have few graphics or reading guides for students. Some language arts publications use a linguistic approach to reading, whereas others use a literature base, a "look-say" method, or a stronger phonics approach. Some math materials are standard texts with lots of skill and drill, whereas others emphasize an application-oriented, concept-based approach. In addition to the more traditional bound materials, some teachers use a wealth of online learning tools. These tools are of high interest to some learners because they relay information through nontraditional media.

Changing resources is a common practice in classrooms where differentiated instruction is the goal. This technique often encompasses the use of multiple resources, including informational texts, narrative texts, multimedia resources, and human resources—each of which offers a different dynamic to the teaching-learning process of gathering, analyzing, interpreting, and applying incoming information in relevant ways.

Informational Texts

Effective PLC teams gather materials that offer a range of difficulty, a spectrum of views, and a diversity of media. First among the categories of differentiated resources are the informational texts that are, more often than not, abundant in schools—though the point must be made that some schools of poverty need textbooks of any kind. Regardless, schools need a variety of texts to meet student readiness levels.

In addition to the standard textbooks, however, PLC teams can add to their resources for particular units of study by using essays, articles, research journals, newspapers, and a multitude of online resources including frequently updated websites that are readily accessed for inquiring groups. The information society is steeped with these informational resources.

Narrative Texts

While narrative texts serve particular purposes in the literature classroom, they are also grand resources for other subject areas. The science class can explore science fiction media, and the history class can examine historical novels, for example. In addition to novels and stories, narrative texts include scripts, daily newspaper columns, opinion pages, editorials, autobiographies, biographies, and memoirs. Personal blogs add interesting texture, though they may have more appeal to certain kinds of learners who take in information as fast as they can. However, caution is recommended about monitoring the appropriateness, the credibility, the reliability, and the validity of the sources.

Multimedia Resources

While online learning resources have been mentioned previously, multimedia resources are essential for developing 21st century skills. PLCs focused on collaboration, students, and student results are hooked in, linked in, and often swept into myriad media and online opportunities.

These media modes range from DVDs to podcasts, from television to YouTube, from books on tape to voice-activated Web searches. They can be found on computers in labs and classrooms and in the handheld devices that students have with them at all times. There is no way out of this maze of media frenzy, and tech-savvy PLCs have a distinct advantage over those without experience with technology. The media available and accessible to students are well known and well worn by them. The teaching staff are the ones trying to catch up, and the PLC teams willing and able to share techno-knowledge and techno-resources will be doing the entire staff a huge and invaluable favor.

Human Resources

When PLC teams talk about changing the content by changing the resources, they must also include human resources. There is not a more valued or frequently used resource than other human beings. "Hey, how do you spell *mnemonic*?" "What was the name of that website on cardiovascular stats for exercise?" "Where can I find that recipe?" There is no end to the stream of information gleaned from a knowing colleague.

While these kinds of questions may seem like informal, everyday interactions, human resources can also be tapped through more formal means, such as face-to-face interviews, online interviews, Web chats and discussion threads, interactive blogs, and guest panels presenting varying viewpoints. Human resources are also used in team meetings, peer dialogues, teacher-led conferences, and small-group investigations and discussions. Some learners are interpersonal and auditory by learning preference. These students particularly need human interaction to learn, though all students benefit from human interaction as a resource option.

Level of Information

To best serve students, teachers need to also be aware of the level of the content. At the middle and high school levels, for instance, some publishers write texts with built-in cues and clues to escort the reader through new vocabulary and difficult concepts. Other texts read more like college-level materials that can be fairly incomprehensible to the struggling learner, but a welcome challenge to the advanced student. PLC teams will become resourceful in finding various levels of text to use with their students.

Remember, working in PLCs is always about learning new ways to approach the students. The focus should be on collaboration for student success and desired results. Skillful teachers use an array of resource levels, matching learners and methods along the way, and welcome the opportunity to converse in teams to share ideas and options to renew and refresh their teaching repertoires.

In sum, these resources are familiar to some and foreign to others. Through a learning community, this warehouse of options can become visible and accessible to all the teachers on the team. Their efforts are rewarded again and again as they continue on their path to becoming highly functioning teams of professionals.

At the end of this chapter (page 73), you'll find more elementary, middle, and high school examples of changing the resources.

Changing the Environment

Changing the learning environment is yet another method of differentiating the content. Learning environments include not only the classroom environment, but also the school, the neighborhood, the community, and even the virtual environment of technology. In essence, by changing the learning environment, the content inherently changes as well.

One brief example illustrates changing content by changing the environment. Imagine a middle school student learning about trout fishing through a reading program. Then, imagine the same student learning about trout fishing on a fishing trip with his grandfather. Finally, imagine that student learning about trout fishing by watching the film *A River Runs Through It* at the community movie theater. In each instance, the student is learning similar content, but in an environment that dictates a particular perspective on that content.

Now, look at a more academic type of content: grades 4 through 6 study simple machines. While learning about the six simple machines (pulley, lever, inclined plane, wedge, wheel, and screw), students are invited to work with the content in several different learning environments. They may choose to work in the classroom, building Rube Goldberg inventions that incorporate the simple machines. They may decide to work in the resource center, researching simple machines and the principles of physics that apply to the simple machines. They may elect to work with a community business or industry partner, investigating how simple machines are applied to more sophisticated machines in a real machine shop. Or they may explore the concept of simple machines by searching the Internet for an appropriate software application. In all of the experiences, learners are being exposed to the concepts and principles operating in simple machines, yet each of the situations provides particular contexts that impact learning.

Changing the environment changes how the learner experiences the topic or theme being studied. Just by virtue of being in a different environment, the student learns about the subject matter quite differently. Although the idea of changing the learning environment seems like a lot of work for teachers, many unsuspected opportunities present themselves after teachers start thinking about learning environments.

Environment options encompass a number of different, but readily available, settings that provide opportunities for differentiation. PLC teams can use each of the following learning environments—classrooms, school buildings, neighborhoods, communities, and virtual classrooms—to stretch their thinking about differentiating instruction.

Classrooms

The classroom is the natural environment for learning. Of course, this includes the many and varied classrooms that students inhabit. In the elementary classroom, a student's classroom is home. These classrooms are alive—plants on the windowsills, learning corners with books and pillows, technology centers, and bulletin boards strewn with student work, large letters, and learning slogans. Rich in texture and tone, elementary classrooms present a climate for learning that is inviting to all and conducive to differentiated instruction. Teachers can change the environment for learning just by having students occupy various corners (working at the writing center versus at the teacher's table) or areas (working on the rug versus at the desk), or even by changing levels (working under the table versus at the table). The options are many within the single classroom.

For the middle and high school students, one classroom is home base with many other classrooms slotted for daily visits. Each has its own learning environment crafted for the specific learning that occurs there: art rooms filled with supplies, shelves, and student portfolios of work; science classrooms filled with smells, beakers, and element charts; social studies classrooms filled with maps, globes, and interactive whiteboards; music classrooms filled with a piano, a multitude of other instruments, music stands, and sheet music. There is no single classroom that provides everything needed for the comprehensive middle or high school curriculum, yet the learning environments in each room are diverse, relevant, and ripe for differentiation.

School Buildings

In addition to the various classrooms, the entire school building offers many possibilities for differentiating the learning environment. Teachers have countless options to vary the learning environment for specific students and for particular purposes, from hallways and storerooms to study carrels and offices; from libraries and media centers to computer labs and custodian rooms; from lunchrooms and auditoriums to "cafetoriums" and center stage. Creative teaching staff use these nooks and crannies, because they provide secluded areas for small group discussions, team projects, reading quietly, and even conferencing with teams. Sharing ideas such as these in the PLC teams guarantees relevant differentiation.

Neighborhoods

While elementary teachers seem to use the neighborhood for various activities from poetry reading under the old oak tree to nature walks, civic cleanups, rock collecting, and leaf identification, the middle and high school teachers seem less inclined to participate in the rich environments that surround the school. By differentiating the learning environment, however, teachers have a powerful tool to motivate and involve students.

Communities

Community field trips for big kids and little kids provide genuine, authentic experiences proven to be extremely powerful learning environments. In fact, when thinking about the impact of brain science on learning, Diamond and Hopson (1998) advocate rich and robust environments that provide appropriate and varied sensory stimuli and the time to interact intensely within that setting. In addition, some teachers advocate—for the sake of students lacking in background experiences and prior knowledge—the annual field trip at the beginning of the year, so those powerfully deep experiences can be referenced all year.

These community excursions are not just for the younger students. Older students truly benefit when they visit businesses, conduct interviews, tour facilities, practice career skills, and understand the workings of the transit system, local government, businesses, and industries that serve their community. The options are incredible as PLC teams put their heads together and pool ideas for their students. It is this kind of brainstorming session that moves the PLC to think outside of the box. This is where differentiated instruction gets exciting. It is also during these dynamic sessions that adult learning and the sense of "teamness" are at their peak.

Community field trips for elementary students often include the zoo, circus, farm, firehouse, police station, or particular museums and galleries in the area. Middle and high school students visit the courthouse, local paper factory, or automotive facility. They might go to the local newspaper office or television studio, a stage play, a symphony performance, or even the opera. On these community excursions, students are sometimes given opportunities to interact with vibrant entities in the area, as part of the projects they undertake in their various courses. These experiences help build rich background knowledge for students lacking in authentic life experience.

Virtual Classrooms

In an entirely different realm, teachers can change the learning environment with virtual field trips, guided discussion questions, and site monitoring, of course. When PLC teams manage this option of virtual field trips appropriately and assertively, it has unbelievable impact. In fact, Chenoweth (2009) illustrates how one school in Falls Church, Virginia, uses this differentiation option as a vital part of building background knowledge for students who may be deficient in a certain subject area or unit of study:

> Graham Road [Elementary School] teachers use thousands of documentary videos that many schools can access. If they want children to read a particular book but they know they won't understand the references to earthquakes and volcanoes, they have students visit the "background knowledge center," otherwise known as the computer. (p. 40)

In closing, purposeful use of myriad areas of the classroom and of the many learning spaces throughout the school building itself provide fertile ground for learning environments. Field trips in the neighborhood and the community, as well as to virtual environments, round out the multitude of choices PLC teams have as they support differentiated instruction by changing the learning environment.

Examples of Changing the Content

Following are elementary, middle, and high school examples of changing the complexity of the content, changing the resources that present content, and changing the learning environment of the content.

Elementary School Examples

Changing the complexity: *Buoyancy*

- Concrete—Test various objects to see whether they sink or float.
- Symbolic—View videos and draw diagrams of floating objects.
- Abstract—Read texts or listen to lectures on buoyancy.

Changing the resources: *Presidential election*

- Informational—Read a chapter about presidential elections; read primary historical newspaper sources related to past presidencies; read about Washington or Lincoln.
- Narrative—Analyze a political cartoon depicting a presidential act.
- Multimedia—Watch a documentary or fictional film with a presidential theme; study the official executive branch of government website.
- Human resources—Interview a local politician about election procedures.

Changing the learning environment: *Life cycle*

- Classroom—Grow plants in various areas of the classroom.

- School building—Plan and create a natural prairie in a designated area of the schoolyard.

- Neighborhood—Visit an arboretum or a conservatory to experience the life cycle of plants.

Middle School Examples

Changing the complexity: *Pre-algebra*

- Concrete—Use hands-on learning stations to manipulate objects that depict an equation sentence.

- Symbolic—Draw graphs to represent equations as a pictorial checking method.

- Abstract—Solve an equation with the help of a textbook, and create equations for others to solve.

Changing the resources: *Biology/DNA*

- Informational—Read a text on Crick and Watson's discovery.

- Narrative—Read the novel *My Sister's Keeper* by Jodi Picoult.

- Multimedia—Use a Web-based program to develop profiles of students' inherited traits.

- Human resources—Interview doctors at a local hospital about genetic data management.

Changing the learning environment: *World history*

- Classroom—Create a "War Room" center for role-play on decision making.

- School building—Use the multimedia center to create research reports.

- Neighborhood—Visit local cemetery sites of war heroes.

- Community—Visit a veterans hospital and interview a soldier or nurse.

- Virtual classroom—Access war stories, war documentaries, or war museums online.

High School Examples

Changing the complexity: *American literature*

- Concrete—Gather and collect Americana objects that represent the American dream, and assemble these into a table-sized sculpture.

- Symbolic—Create a graphic-organizer web of the American dream.

- Abstract—Read a 19th- and a 20th-century novel to compare and contrast the American dream depiction in each.

Changing the resources—*World geography*

- Informational—Compare atlases, globes, general maps, and paleographic maps.

- Narrative—Read period novels, short stories, and poetry focusing on places around the world.

- Multimedia—Review Internet aerial views, GPS technology, scale drawings with CAD/CAM software, cartography artifacts, web links, and blogs such as the following:

    + All Points Blog (www.allpointsblog.com)

    + All Things Geography (http://allthingsgeography.blogspot.com)

    + Digital Earth (www.digitalearth.com.au)

    + GPS Tracklog (http://gpstracklog.com)

    + Google Maps Mania (http://googlemapsmania.blogspot.com)

    + Great Map (http://greatmap.blogspot.com)

    + Mapping Hacks (http://mappinghacks.com)

    + The Map Room (www.mcwetboy.net/maproom)

    + Very Spatial (http://veryspatial.com)

    + Webmapper (www.webmapper.net)

- Human resources—Interview local meteorologists, pilots, business owners, bankers, and salesmen about their training and professions.

Changing the learning environment: *Business math*

- Classroom—Use classroom computers to learn Excel and QuickBooks.

- School building—Visit the main office or department offices to learn about budgets and strategic planning.

- Neighborhood—Visit banks for interest data, stores for comparative shopping, and corner sites to survey foot traffic.

- Community—Visit business and industry locations for internships and interview opportunities.

- Virtual classroom—Use the Internet to study stocks and bonds in real time; use web stats to track web traffic and demographic marketing information as well as statistical analyses.

Action Options

"What content are we going to teach? What do we want students to learn?" These are the fundamental questions that teachers in PLCs ask themselves as they prepare for class. The content, as it relates to learning standards, is articulated in government documents approved at the state level, and the PLC teams will have already decided the essential power standards. The content remains constant, but how that content is presented is as varied as the imaginations of the skilled classroom teachers. Changing the content in a differentiated classroom means changing the complexity of the content, the resources used to teach the content, and the learning environment where the teaching of the content takes place.

The Action Options in this chapter highlight several exercises connected to changing the complexity, resources, and environment. We include four activities for PLC teams to try as they become more familiar with the idea of explicitly changing the content to target learner needs. The first, In Thirty-Three Words, is a brief synopsis activity; the second centers on the idea of tiered lessons; the third is a brainstorming activity called Acronym Graffiti; and the fourth, Color Coding, is an activity designed to make sense of plan books with an eye for differentiation. All four strategies foster deeper understanding of the discussion presented in this chapter. Be sure to check out www.allthingsplc.info/wordpress/?p=69 for a discussion on how schools are differentiating content in a standards-based curriculum.

Action Option 1: In Thirty-Three Words

Participants respond to a prompt, writing for a few minutes, using complete sentences. The trick is that participants are only allowed to use thirty-three words total, no more, no less. Try it now. (This paragraph totals thirty-three words.)

In doing this activity, the facilitator provides a prompt focusing on a specific topic, such as *changing the content*, and instructs the team to explore the topic within the strict requirement of thirty-three words. It is much like the parameters of 140 characters for tweets (a form of short emails sent to a limited network of Twitter users). When used in the classroom, the word limit helps students learn to comply with requirements in projects and performances. For example, the teacher may use the prompt *civil rights* to flesh out content on a social studies unit on government.

Action Option 2: Tiered Lesson Stations

Another way a PLC can become more familiar with differentiation is to plan, as a team, a tiered lesson that changes the complexity of the content. To begin, each member takes two pieces of paper and jots down a possible subject matter on each that the PLC could use to plan a tiered lesson. The facilitator places all of the slips of paper in a basket, and members pick one each at random.

Using this randomly selected topic, the team designs a lesson that differentiates the content with three levels of complexity: concrete (hands-on), symbolic (representational drawings), and abstract (text or ideas). By working together, focusing on the same topic, and using the explanations and examples in this chapter as guides, teachers should be able to complete this exercise with some sense of success.

In addition, this exercise can be repeated: instead of changing the complexity of the content, the PLC teams can work on changing the resource or the environment. It doesn't take long before teachers see how natural it is for them to make these adjustments to their lesson designs. Often, they realize that in many situations, they've already been doing these kinds of changes without explicitly accounting for it in their plan books. To make differentiation efforts deliberate and anticipated, the PLC could create a schedule: one week they can look at changing complexity; the next, resources; the next, environment; and finally, all three. What perfect tasks for a teaching community of adult learners!

Action Option 3: Acronym Graffiti

In this high-energy activity, the teachers in PLC teams work in pairs to develop an acronym for a target word. This is a quick, fun, effective way to unpack an idea and illuminate its essence. PLC teams can even make a contest out of it to see which team completes the acronym in the shortest time. It also serves as a great session starter.

Participants use each letter to brainstorm possible resources available for students or have students do this in small groups. In the following example, *environment* is used as the target word in order to get teams thinking about the varied learning environments available:

- Entranceway between the inner and outer doors of the building
- Nooks and crannies in the classroom
- Vast grounds of the schoolyard
- Inside storage rooms
- Resource rooms
- Outside in the park

- **N**ear the office
- **M**akeshift study carrel
- **E**xit areas
- **N**ext to the library
- **T**eacher's workroom

While this may seem a bit frivolous, it's just the kind of outside-the-box thinking that generates differentiated options for instruction. As in all brainstorms, there is a need to revisit the ideas generated and decide which ones are doable. Not all brainstormed ideas are as valued as others once it gets down to implementation, yet the brainstorm often yields unique, relevant ideas. Brainstorming gets ideas flowing and often leads to fresh thinking on old issues. Also, remember that the target word can be any word that PLC teams want to highlight. And, of course, the options for classroom application opportunities are many.

Action Option 4: Color Coding

Color Coding is an exercise that PLC teams can agree to do as a team effort or that individual teachers can do by themselves. To begin, a simple color code is devised to designate places in the plan book that demonstrate opportunities to change the content for learners: for instance, red dots indicate changing the complexity, blue dots indicate changing the resources, and green dots indicate changing the learning environment.

By color coding their plan books even just for a month or so, teachers emphasize their differentiation efforts and can self-evaluate their progress. They can also jigsaw their coding practices by selecting one area to concentrate on each week: week one, complexity; week two, resources; week three, environment; and week four, all three.

If PLC teams decide that all teachers will color code, they can debrief and compile lists for specific differentiation ideas that teachers have used successfully in the past. This is another collegial conversation that cements the concept of differentiated instruction in practical terms.

CHAPTER 5

CHANGING THE PROCESS

PLC TAKE AWAY

Learning How Teachers Differentiate Learning Processes to
Meet Student Needs

This chapter is designed to parallel chapter 4 on changing the content. The ensuing discussion delineates the many ways teams within professional learning communities can modify, adjust, and change the processes students engage in, in order to learn the required content.

Changing the process of learning is one of Tomlinson's (2005) stated strategies for differentiating instruction. As teachers seek ways to change the learning opportunities with challenge and choice, three areas offer fertile ground for substantive differentiation of the process: (1) changing the various aspects of direct instruction, (2) changing the structure of cooperative interactions, or (3) changing the mode of inquiry.

The following synopsis offers an introductory look at these three distinct learning processes. We then break down each process for PLCs to explore more fully. In fact, we designed chapters 4–6 to provide real fodder for collegial conversations that lead to purposeful and meaningful differentiated instruction. It is in these discussions, and the accompanying Action Options, that the ideas of the book come alive for authentic implementation purposes.

Along with these robust discussions about helping teachers change the process, we provide examples for elementary, middle, and high school settings. PLCs can use this chapter as a pivot point for supporting differentiated instruction by changing the learning process. They can compile a bank of ideas for teachers to use intermittently as they plan and design differentiated interactions that include direct instruction, cooperative structures, and student inquiry, thereby building their teaching repertoires.

Direct Instruction Methods

The direct instruction model is sometimes referred to as "stand and deliver." It represents the traditional image of the teacher standing in front of the room, instructing students. While teachers favor direct instruction, especially at the upper levels, researchers and writers in the field of education consider it a lesser model of sound pedagogy. However, when done well within the research-based structures of Hunter (1971) and others, direct instruction methodology is a highly efficient means of imparting information, and some students learn quite readily in this way. There are many ways to differentiate the elements of this time-honored method to make it more effective in reaching all students, including following good lesson design, scaffolding and chunking, whole-class input, small-group input, individual input, and revisiting, reviewing, reteaching, and revising.

Following Good Lesson Design

Changing the method of direct instruction is something that most teachers already do naturally. Madeline Hunter (1971) identified seven elements of a good lesson design:

1 Anticipatory set—motivational introduction, the "hook"

2 Learning objectives—goals of the lesson, standards addressed

3 Input—instructions, information, data, concepts, skills, attitudes

4 Modeling—demonstration of the skill or concept

5 Guided practice—student exercises monitored with feedback from teacher

6 Feedback—specific, immediately relevant comments to students

7 Independent practice—student execution on their own

To change the direct instruction model, shift the order of the elements or the way in which they are used, depending on the circumstances. For example, the teacher may do the input before talking about the learning objectives. In a lesson on magnets, she may discuss magnetic forces and later state the objective of the science unit.

The lesson elements represent the science of teaching, whereas changes in how teachers use the elements represent the art of teaching. Creative teachers in PLC teams craft lessons that are unique and inviting to students. Teams present concepts, skills, and attitudes in lesson designs that create moments of surprise, intrigue, and inquiry. They also change how they involve students in authentic ways prior to, during, and after the learning.

Effective teachers find creative ways to get the focused attention of students by changing the *anticipatory set*. They find that unique methods build student anticipation and entice students into learning. For instance, they might use a cartoon, a riddle, a challenging problem, a game, a compelling story, a surprise guest, a walk, an interview, a video piece, or a poem as effective methods to develop an anticipatory set or an inviting way to hook students into the lesson.

These teachers also make the *learning objective* explicit. In fact, teachers in PLCs clearly articulate it when they converse about lessons. They use different ways of making the purpose of the lesson clear and obvious to students. They may post the objective on the board, tell the students what they will learn that day, or even elicit from the students—following the lesson—what the students see as the lesson goal or what they think the Take Away is for the lesson.

Effective teachers change the *input* by using a repertoire of methodologies to get information across to students. These craftsmen use lectures and mini-lectures, of course, but they also *model* the learning by demonstrating the desired goals and outcomes, and they sample products or performances to indicate the quality of the work expected.

Effective teachers change the *practice* as well. They know how to shift the skill-and-drill kinds of guided practice toward compelling contests, games, and relays. They know how to structure practices that are focused and brief and others that are intensely involved. They know how to utilize practice time with student partners, pairs, and trios as well as time to work independently or with the teacher, an aid, or a peer providing guidance.

Effective teachers also know when and how to give appropriate, timely, and specific *feedback* to reinforce student work. They use many methods of informative assessments to provide optimal feedback about students' efforts on an ongoing basis. They develop checklists or scoring rubrics with quality indicators to guide the student work.

These teachers know how to design *independent practice* as homework assignments that require thought and care in addition to in-school assignments that help students try things out on their own. They provide the needed scaffolding and chunking to make these independent sessions successful for students.

Scaffolding and Chunking

When teachers couple scaffolding and chunking with what is known about the brain and learning, the direct instruction model becomes stronger and more effective. By scaffolding the lesson input, teachers provide the step-by-step construction of the concept or skill that brings the student along a logical pathway toward the end goal. It's kind of like teaching young ones to write a sentence. First students learn the words—nouns and verbs, *rabbit* and *run*. Then they put them together—rabbit runs. Eventually they add adjectives and adverbs, *white* and *fast*, and string them together—white rabbit runs fast. While this is a simple example of scaffolding learning, it is the same process algebra teachers use as they build an equation. Quality teachers excel at the skill of scaffolding. They know how to take things apart and build them up, with logic that students can follow with ease.

Likewise, when teachers integrate chunking techniques into their direct instruction lessons, they address another aspect of brain science that states learning is achieved through patterning (Pete & Fogarty, 2007). Chunking connects key ideas so they bind together in the mind of the learner. When the learner takes in information, the brain searches for a pattern it can fit in, by both enhancing existing patterns and creating new patterns. That's where the critical synaptic connections are made, where the dendrites grow and connect. That is how we learn and retain information. In this way, the concepts are retrieved as a chunk—a set of ideas that have meaning and make sense to the learner.

Teachers include chunking as part of the direct instruction lesson when they stir up prior knowledge. By surfacing what students already know about the topic or idea, teachers can then connect the new, incoming information to that background knowledge. By so doing, they create a chunk of information that stays together as one idea. For effective teachers, tapping into what students bring to the learning situation is a central skill; PLC team members enhance direct instruction with a solid understanding of cognitive science and a differentiation element as they develop lesson plans together.

Whole-Class Input

Whole-class instruction is controversial at best—it works for some students in viable ways, but leaves others by the wayside—yet it is a model that has stood the test of time. However, whole-class instruction is most certainly enhanced by a differentiated approach to instruction. Simply put, when the teacher is planning a whole-group lesson, whether it is built for one class period or several, the lesson is enhanced when presented with at least three modalities. For example, a whole-group lesson may have auditory input (lecture or sharing), visual supports (illustrations or video), and hands-on experiences (manipulatives or model building). In this way, the lesson taps into the differing learning styles and strengths of the students.

Small-Group Input

Differentiating direct instruction with small groups of students is the heart and soul of the differentiated classroom.

Teachers in PLCs use their student achievement data to form flexible skill groups. These data-driven groups are formed based on a known deficit skill area, given intense explicit instructional intervention to remedy the situation as quickly as possible, and carefully monitored for progress. Teachers test students after several weeks of small-group interventions and move them out of the group as deemed appropriate by the test results. In essence, these are not the permanent, homogeneous groups of tracked or streamed classrooms, but rather changing groups that emerge and dissolve as needed.

Flexible skill grouping is a powerful differentiation tool when executed and implemented well with the support of the PLC. PLC teams have the information, the resources, and the know-how to manage these flexible skill groups because they are able to use all of their pooled talents. In fact, these flexible skill groups epitomize the culture and spirit of PLC teams because in creating them, teachers must focus on the essential questions: What do we want students to learn? How will we know they know it? What will we do when they don't?

Forming and monitoring flexible skill groups is a major mission of high-functioning PLC teams looking out for students and fostering student success. This type of grouping provides a viable method to address student needs in the various subject and skill areas. In fact, flexible skill grouping is part of the response to intervention (RTI) movement that addresses the issue of ensuring student success through appropriate progress monitoring and speedy and specified instructional interventions.

Another example of how PLC teams work well to support the flexible small-group work is tied directly to common assessments. As the teams examine data on student achievement from the common assessments, they emerge with a clear picture of which students are excelling and which need specific instructional attention. This additional attention may come in the form of reteaching the concept in general or targeting particular skill development for the designated group of students. In any case, the team approach to these decisions supports both the students and the teachers who work for student success.

Individual Input

The idea of progress monitoring and instant interventions leads directly to individual attention for a student who exhibits a need for instructional help of some kind. There is simply no instruction more powerful or impactful than one-to-one tutoring (Bloom, 1956). When the teacher has the opportunity to work with an individual student, the intensity, the tailoring, and the time spent pays off. Students often learn readily in these tutorials because the teacher gains insight into the challenges or problem areas easier than with large- or small-group work. It's simple for kids to hide out in groups, but with the teacher-student interaction, they are in the spotlight. There is no match to this kind of coaching support; it is a primary tool of PLC teams as they assemble a bank of strategies to ensure success for every student.

Revisiting, Reviewing, Reteaching, and Revising

Our discussion of direct instruction would not be complete without a nod to the ideas of revisiting, reviewing, reteaching, and revising (Pete & Fogarty, 2005):

- Revisiting—a brief touchback; references that "spiral through the day"
- Reviewing—a five-minute look back at key ideas, skills, or procedures
- Reteaching—a completely new lesson; same topic, new and different approach
- Revising—a chance to note and correct for accuracy

These are natural scaffolding techniques of the skillful teacher and ripe topics of conversation for the collegial sessions within the PLC teams.

Revisiting means orchestrating a brief touchback to the original learning. In a revisiting strategy, teachers may reference the idea of skill throughout the day or the discussion as a reminder. Revisiting is a quick brain-friendly strategy that keeps the ideas under study front and center all day. For example, in fourth-grade math, if the topic is fractions, the teacher might say, just before lunch, "Don't forget to eat a large fraction of your healthy lunch items." Before dismissing her fourth graders for the day, she might add, "For homework tonight, I want you to do all of it, not a fraction of it." It sounds silly, but the effect is lasting. The brain is given a chance to think about the idea intermittently, which has an impact (Pete & Fogarty, 2005).

Reviewing calls a little more attention and time to the original learning; typically, the teacher takes a few moments at the beginning of the next lesson to review the previously presented information. It's a reboot, catch-up, or tips-to-remember time before new information is loaded on. This might be a five- to ten-minute look back at key ideas, skills, or procedures. It may evolve from the homework review as students express challenges they had, or it may just be a teacher-directed review of critical components.

For example, the teacher may ask students to review the three states of matter by working with a partner and doing a "Tell and Retell" activity. One student defines the three states of matter, while the partner retells the same information in his or her own words. It's quick and effective because they support each other by reinforcing the key ideas. Such a review would take between five and eight minutes, including a teacher sampling at the end.

Reteaching is another direct instruction strategy that enhances the original lesson. Reteaching uses a completely new lesson to cover the same topic with a new and different approach. It differentiates for the entire group because the teacher approaches the information from a different perspective, medium, or place. This backup lesson can cement the learning.

For example, a middle school teacher may want to reinforce key facts from Jennifer Lindsay's (2000) book on Jane Goodall and gorillas in the wild. To approach this in a way other than the reading-discussion model, she directs students to create individual mind maps of the facts to date and then has them share their maps with a partner. She uses a new approach to the material, and she gets a sense of where students are in their understanding.

The last element that reinforces a direct instruction lesson is the *revising* strategy. When teachers revise ideas, based on the work students submit, the teachers have a rare and cherished chance to note inaccuracies, misconceptions, and misunderstandings. This is their opportunity to correct the mistakes. The revision part of direct instruction ensures everyone understands with accuracy and precision.

For instance, a high school physics teacher has students pair up, compare homework problems, and talk about any differences in answers. She asks them to look at each other's strategies and check for the correct answers. Then, she models the right answers as well as how to obtain them through the process previously taught. Just because she taught it once doesn't mean the students caught it. Imagine the wealth of ideas shared and the stories told in PLC teams as they talk about revising instruction for lost or misinformed students.

In closing, direct instruction is a viable method with many opportunities for differentiating that instruction through whole-group, flexible skill groups, or one-to-one direct instruction. When teachers follow good lesson design, use scaffolding and chunking techniques, and offer tutorial and coaching support, the direct instruction model offers plenty of opportunities for team collaboration.

See the end of this chapter (page 94) for elementary, middle, and high school examples of changing the process with direct instruction elements.

Cooperative Learning Methods

A second major method for changing the process of instruction is differentiation through the many models of classroom collaborations, commonly collected under the heading of cooperative learning. Our discussion examines five elements that distinguish cooperative learning groups from other small-group work and delineates the decisions teachers make as they design cooperative interactions.

As a pedagogical method, cooperative learning has a long and interesting historical context, and the recognition and acknowledgment of its power as a learning technique continues to this day. The research on cooperative learning goes back to the 1970s with David and Roger Johnson's writings (see Johnson, Johnson, & Holubeck, 1986). Cooperative learning as a differentiation strategy is still an urgent topic of conversation within PLCs because it is considered highly effective in increasing student achievement (Bellanca & Fogarty, 2003; Johnson et al., 1996; Joyce & Showers, 2002; Kagan, 1994; Marzano, Pickering, & Pollock, 2001). Unfortunately, this is an underused strategy, particularly in the upper grade levels. It's the task of the teams within these communities to find ways to make cooperative learning an integral strategy of the differentiated classroom.

Five Critical Elements

The five critical elements in the BUILD strategy that distinguish cooperative learning from small-group work include (Bellanca & Fogarty, 2003, p. 56):

1. Building in higher-order thinking (predicting, analyzing, concluding)

2. Uniting the team (specifying team roles and responsibilities, team tasks, and team rewards)

3. Including individual accountability (requiring personal responsibility for the information)

4. Looking back and reflecting (learning about collaborative work)

5. Developing social skills (focusing on communication, leadership, and teamwork)

When structured with these five elements, small-group work becomes cooperative learning, because it has the structures in place to guide quality teamwork and to ensure development of social interactions among students. For example, to build higher-order thinking—the B of BUILD—the teacher can ask students to make a prediction; for the U, uniting all members of the team, teachers may assign specific roles for members of the group (recorder, reporter, manager). For the I in BUILD, individual accountability, the teacher can require an individual assignment; to help students look back and reflect—the L—the teacher may ask students what was hard and what was easy about the task. In addition, teachers may implicitly target a developing social skill (taking turns, accepting ideas, encouraging others)—the D of BUILD. It takes time to become proficient at quality cooperative tasks, but as this strategy becomes integrated with direct instruction models, both teachers and students learn the techniques that make it work.

Teacher Decisions

In order to provide the necessary structure for cooperative groups, teachers must make a number of decisions every time they use cooperative learning. While these decisions seem cumbersome at first, they become easier over time as students familiarize themselves with the cooperative learning model. Following are some of the choices teachers discuss within the PLC teams as they develop the best instructional methods for using cooperative learning.

Number of Students

Teachers decide on the number of students in a group and the makeup or composition of the group. We recommend heterogeneous groups, because the more diverse the group, the richer the product. The differentiation goal is to change the process by incorporating various cooperative structures, which range from duos to trios to small groups. While these are not new ideas, it seems prudent to revisit them here to encourage more frequent and customized use of cooperative constructs, because of the strong research supporting this strategy (Bellanca & Fogarty, 2003).

Duos are one of the most powerful cooperative structures for the classroom. The "power of two" is in the give and take of the partnership. It's hard to drop out of a twosome because the success of the group depends on the two involved. There is no one else.

A *trio* is a special cooperative strategy that allows for partner interaction with a built-in observer. Alternatively, the threesome might work together as a small group with various roles and responsibilities required to complete the task; for instance, they might have a recorder, a reporter, and a leader. Trios make very effective groupings for students because the small number of participants makes decisions manageable.

Small groups may be used in a more formal setting, with four to five students arranged in a heterogeneous grouping. The roles and responsibilities vary, depending on the complexity of the tasks. With small groups, however, there is a need to incorporate explicit social-skill instruction (Johnson, Johnson, & Holubec, 1986) so students learn how to work effectively together. Small groups are perfect opportunities for students to learn how to reach agreements, listen attentively, and encourage others on the team.

Limitations, Roles, and Responsibilities

Teachers also design the cooperative task and time limit, as well as the roles and responsibilities needed to complete the group task. For example, teachers might tell student teams that they have twenty minutes to complete a concept map on the topic of nutrition. To provide further structure to the group, effective PLC teams should have robust conversations about the various roles and responsibilities they use in the cooperative tasks. They name roles such as materials manager, recorder, reporter, encourager, and traveler. In addition, they get creative; for example, the English teacher talks about how she uses the role of scribe and discussion leader as students work in their novel groups, the math teacher shares his roles of calculator and checker, and the science teacher describes her lab technician and scientist roles. The explicit roles add the structure needed to develop team building and leadership.

Outcome of Interaction

Finally, teachers effectively using cooperative learning decide on the outcome of the interaction: what the product or performance might be, how it will be assessed, and what kind of reflection the team will be required to do. All of these carefully defined structures make the cooperative learning activity bound for success (Bellanca & Fogarty, 2003).

Three specific cooperative strategies in which team members can bounce ideas off of one another about learning outcomes include "Turn to Your Partner and . . . ," Think-Pair-Share, and the Three Musketeers, all of which can be found in the Action Options section (page 96). Remember that PLC teacher teams have a multitude of other structures to share as well.

Inquiry Learning Methods

Student inquiry is a third learning method in which students lead investigations and explorations of various topics. Student inquiry is frequently considered a more student-directed process than the previous two models of direct instruction and cooperative learning. However, it can be introduced and implemented quite successfully in the K–12 setting if the parameters are set and the models have proper scaffolding during rollout of the planning stages. Modes of inquiry have great appeal to certain learning styles and preferences. In fact, many students at every level will execute them with skill and grace. These modes include problem-based learning, service learning, case studies, project learning, and performance learning, each of which are worthy endeavors orchestrated by the leadership of the teachers, but enacted and sometimes directed by the student teams themselves. We've included the research base for each mode, the critical elements that comprise the models, and some examples to review at the various levels.

Some modes of inquiry included in this category are very structured with specific stages and phases of development; others are more open-ended endeavors that allow teachers to determine the required or preferred procedures that give students the opportunity to sort out the steps as they go along.

See the end of this chapter (page 94) for elementary, middle, and high school examples of changing the process with inquiry learning methods.

Structured Inquiry Models

Inquiry learning can become the primary instructional method for the unit or lesson, or it can be an integral part that works in combination with direct instruction and cooperative learning. When teachers change the process to differentiate the instruction with inquiry models, students take on a more proactive role than they do in the direct instruction model or in many cooperative tasks structured for them. Rather than the teacher being responsible for covering content, students become responsible for "uncovering" content; students are at the center of this instructional method. In the following section, we explain three different models of inquiry, beginning with an inviting model called problem-based learning, then moving to the civic-focused instruction of service learning, and finally to moral and ethical issues covered by case studies.

Problem-Based Learning

Grounded in the medical model of Barrows and Tamblyn (1980), problem-based learning is becoming a well-known and often-used model within PLC teams. In this model, students "meet" a real-world problem and are expected to plot a path toward its resolution. Steps to address the problem are delineated as follows:

1 Define the problem.

2 Assume a stakeholder role, and create a scenario and statement.

3 Gather facts, data, and information by following many leads.

4 Analyze, interpret, and make sense of the information.

5 Rephrase the problem.

6 Generate viable alternatives by listening to all ideas in the brainstorming sessions.

7 Decide on the best solution by consensus.

8 Publish the findings for interested and involved parties.

The problem solving begins with students identifying the "real" problem and creating a problem scenario that states an open-ended concern. To give you a brief glimpse at this process, consider a teacher presenting a real-world concern taken from the local newspaper to the students. The problem focuses on a newly constructed high-rise with elevators that were too slow; there were many complaints from the new commercial tenants. Student discussions lead to a scenario and statement of the problem as they define it. In this way, the students take ownership of the problem and become troubleshooters who tackle the challenge. More specifically, the problem-based learning scenario begins with a statement naming a stakeholder role, then states the problem, and ends with an open-ended question, such as the following:

> You are the developers of a new high-rise that has just been completed. The tenants are commercial businesses and all leases are signed and the occupancy is in its final stages. However, tenants are disgruntled because of insufficient elevator service and are flooding your office with complaints. What will you do?

Students initially identify the problem as slow elevators. Along the way, of course, students engage in research tasks, interviews, and investigations (Fogarty, 1997). The students use all of their human and virtual resources to find out about the building itself, through the Internet and news articles. They learn about the construction process of skyscrapers and the cost factors involved. They contact tenants and conduct remote phone interviews and email interviews. They do a thorough search for pertinent information, sometimes working in teams and sharing the tasks among the various team members in a jigsaw model.

After much reporting back, with robust analyses and comprehensive interpretations of the situation, the students turn the discussion to possible, probable, or preferred alternatives. In the course of the brainstorming, many valid and many wild ideas surface, including the following:

- Reset elevator schedules and speeds.
- Limit the elevators. Have certain elevators service certain floors.
- Send a note to the tenants proposing a schedule for various offices.
- Install escalators.
- Have helicopter service from the rooftop.
- Fix the new elevators.
- Reduce and limit the number of offices with tenants.
- Put mirrors on the walls by the elevators.

When that last idea is floated, the students question the logic of mirrors. They ask the student offering this idea what mirrors have to do with the elevator problem. He defends his idea by explaining that he reframed the problem:

> The problem is not about the slow elevators, it is about the disgruntled tenants. If we put mirrors on the walls by all of the elevators, the tenants will be so busy looking at

themselves in the mirrors, they won't be upset about the wait. They won't notice it so much. I've seen it many times in the tall buildings downtown. It's just common sense.

In this little example, the students decide, quite astutely, to identify the real problem—disgruntled tenants; in doing so, they have come up with a viable and cost-effective solution. Students zero in on the mirror idea and prepare their findings for a public presentation. It takes the problem-based learning experience full circle.

This problem-based learning example illustrates the real-world aspect of inquiry learning. In other situations, PLC teams might choose to address an environmental issue or a sociological concern of some sort: local ordinances, school issues, or even global concerns. Whatever the focus, problem-based learning usually begins with "You are . . . " thus establishing the student's role as stakeholder, and ends with the explicitly open-ended "What will you do?," so the problem statement does not lead the students to a premature answer. It is a motivating model for students, especially those who are self-directed.

Service Learning

Service learning is about immersion in an experience as a way to investigate and learn from real-world situations. It links service to others with existing goals in the curriculum. It is sometimes implemented as a senior project, and may even be tied to graduation requirements. Service learning is also a viable inquiry model for upper elementary, middle, and high school students, however.

The service-learning model has a formal structure with five elements:

1 Selecting the need for service

2 Finding a community partner

3 Aligning the service experience to educational goals

4 Managing the project

5 Fostering reflective learning

In a way, the service-learning model epitomizes John Dewey's experiential learning theory (1916), which advocates for learning in the real world as well as in the classroom setting.

Service learning is usually aligned to a community or civic concern. It might include students working with a neighborhood senior center and interacting with the residents, or it might focus on neighborhood beautifications, community fundraisers, or political surveys. While this mode of learning requires a good deal of teacher involvement, the more opportunities students have to give service to the community, the easier those projects become. With repeated projects, the student benefits also become more obvious. In the end, it can be an extraordinary curricular option.

Case Studies

Case studies also provide a chance for inquiry (Fogarty, 1997). *Case studies* are narratives or stories of actual situations. The case is presented, and students discuss and debate the moral and ethical issues that emerge as the study unfolds. This inquiry process follows structured phases; teachers should:

1   Share a compelling narrative

2   Help students summarize the facts

3   Focus small-group discussions with key questions

4   Lead a debriefing session with the whole group

5   Provide follow-up readings (recommended)

Case studies involve dilemmas that question moral issues such as dishonesty. For example, is a white lie, such as lying to protect someone's feelings, the same as a lie about something serious, such as stealing? Censorship is another moral dilemma students could grapple with—perhaps exploring why the public library censored a newly released book. Middle school PLC teams developing a lesson on individual rights might use a case study such as the following.

Case Study: Student Rights or School Rights

School officials have conducted a locker search of all middle school students. An upset parent, Mr. Jones, comes to the principal's office and accuses the school leadership of infringing on student rights. Mrs. Smith, the school principal, explains that they are being proactive about the increasing use of drugs by early adolescents, and the search was justified as a "safe schools" measure. Mr. Jones's son, Robert, is embarrassed by the presence of his dad at school, even though his friends think it's cool that his dad is taking their side of the argument. Where do you stand on this issue? Why?

Students might identify with a particular character in the vignette and try to discern the key elements of the situation from that character's point of view. Major components of the inquiry are the ensuing debriefing discussions and the application of the lessons to personally relevant situations.

As a collaborative community, the teams often generate a list of moral dilemmas relevant to their student body. These become fertile ground for relevant inquiry about ethical issues. As such, they can be embraced by every teacher and every student. They provide another dimension to the success story of the students in the group. Just as with the inquiry models of problem-based learning and service learning, case studies are grounded in real-world issues and lead students to examine and confront relevant and timely concerns.

Less-Structured Inquiry Models

Project learning and performance learning are two common models of less-structured inquiry that are popular and effective with students. According to Caine et al. (2009), the activities often considered extracurricular—such as the school year-book, the school newspaper or daily blog, the spring musical, or the holiday art demonstration—should be the centerpiece of the curriculum. These are the authentic project and performance learning models in which students problem solve, make decisions, and create genuine products and performances.

Project Learning

Projects in science, social studies, and the fine and practical arts involve research and investigations centered on the student (Berman, 1999). As stated previously, the project may result in a product or a performance, but it almost always involves real problem solving and decision making. These projects range in time from one class period to several weeks. Sometimes, the project requirements include a report of the findings as well.

The types of projects are unending. Depending on the grade-level curriculum, they might include dioramas in literature class, construction of maps in history, science inventions and collections, math models and statistical graphs, or CAD/CAM drawing in technology class. As PLCs discuss, design, orchestrate, and share their culminating projects or performances, they are energized, and the learning in the group is differentiated in ways that tap into the many talents and needs of students. This kind of action approaches the heart of departmental, grade-level, or interdisciplinary PLC work. Teams become true learning organizations as they intentionally share and compare good techniques and project ideas across the curriculum.

Performance Learning

Performance learning focuses on the design and development of an authentic performance such as a musical production, a dramatic play, a demonstration of the marching band, or practical demonstrations such as gymnastics or cooking shows. The performance becomes the instruction and the assessment all rolled into one.

Students might create PowerPoint presentations, participate on a debate team, or sing in a choral performance. In more involved performances, students may produce a classic play for the community, develop a simulation of a historical event for another class, or sponsor a "court sports" (volleyball, tennis, basketball, dodgeball, calisthenics) demonstration night for parents.

From classroom productions to entire school performances, inquiry learning brings out the best in student learning because the projects are developed with an audience in mind. The stakes are high and the work rigorous. Learning is no longer about inert knowledge; the inquiry process requires true demonstrations of the learning. In addition, inquiry learning is enhanced by the interactions and collegial conversations of professional learning communities at every level of school—elementary, middle, and high school. As the teams develop these projects and performance ideas within the PLC, they end up with a reserve they may want to incorporate in the future.

As stated earlier, these inquiry modes of learning do not have to be the sole instructional models, but can be combined with direct instruction and cooperative models. In fact, the best instructional plans include an assortment of these various methods of changing student learning processes.

Examples of Changing the Process

Following are examples of differentiated instruction via changing the process of learning. Options discussed in this chapter included direct instruction, cooperative learning, and inquiry modes. All levels of schooling are used to exemplify the differentiation process.

Elementary School Examples

Direct instruction: *Vocabulary building*

- Anticipatory set—Decorate shoe boxes for teacher-made word cards by covering the boxes with construction paper or painting them with poster paint.

- Input—Collect teacher-made word cards every day on strips of construction paper.

- Practice—Play Go Fish with a partner using the word cards.

Cooperative learning: *States of matter*

- Duos—Read a picture book together about making pudding.

- Trios—Draw pictures of the three of states of matter.

- Small group—Make instant pudding by shaking the instant powder and milk in a capped plastic bottle.

Inquiry: *Gravity*

- Problem-based learning—Set up story problems for pairs.

- Projects—Build a Rube Goldberg machine that uses gravity to work.

- Performances—Experiment with objects and record findings.

Middle School Examples

Direct instruction: *State government*

- Anticipatory set—Draw a state name from a basket, and research facts about the selected state's government.

- Input—Debrief the branches of government by comparing and contrasting several states.

- Practice—Write quiz about executive, legislative, and judicial branches.

Cooperative learning: *Art*

- Duos—Draw a cartoon character using eight different mediums.

- Trios—Compare and contrast the group's three characters with a triple Venn diagram.

- Small group (of four)—Create a comic strip with all four cartoon characters interacting.

Inquiry: *Black history month*

- Service learning—Paint a mural on the neighborhood underpass wall.

- Projects—Create a collage of African Americans from your region.

- Performances—Perform a first-person autobiographical skit of a famous African American.

High School Examples

Direct instruction: *Metric system*

- Anticipatory set—Use a riddle, cartoon, game, guest, walk, interview, video, or poem to open a unit on the metric system.

- Input—Use problem solving, a lecture, case study, film, field trip, or guest speaker to unpack the metric content.

- Practice—Provide various types of assignments with the metric unit that are focused/brief, intense/longer, or homework.

Cooperative learning: *Expository writing on democracy*

- Duos—Use think-pair-share to brainstorm points of view.

- Trios—Have two partners write while the third observes the editing process.

- Small groups (of four to five)—Work as a team with roles, tasks, and a topic for debate as a prewriting activity on the topic of democracy.

Inquiry: *Stem cell research*

- Problem-based learning—Create a scenario around the issue of stem cell research; include a stakeholder role and an open-ended question (You are . . . You will . . .).

- Case studies—Find case studies of stem cell research to examine the moral and ethical dilemmas of the concept.

- Projects—Assign a project around the topic of stem cell research and require a product or performance.

Action Options

> **PLC TAKE AWAY**
>
> Learning How Teachers Differentiate Learning Processes to Meet Student Needs

PLCs have agreed-upon beliefs that value all aspects of the learning organization. Integral to this culture is the ongoing search for ways to entice students into successful learning experiences through a variety of robust learning options. Risk taking is often connected to these dynamic models of teaching because it requires teachers to think outside the box and move beyond their comfort zones on instructional designs, yet teams of teachers working within PLCs are committed to the ongoing regimen of lifelong learning. They know they must continue to add to their repertoires if they are going to reach every student.

The Action Options in this chapter include Team Names, Tear-Share, "Turn to Your Partner and . . . ," Think-Pair-Share, and the Three Musketeers. Each exercise is intended for PLC teams to use as they learn more about Tomlinson's theory of differentiation; each has potential for classroom interactions to engage learners. Visit the All Things PLC website, www.allthingsplc.info/pdf/links/Overview-PLCatWork .pdf, to read an overview of PLCs as well as about the role of collective inquiry to seek new methods of teaching.

Action Option 1: Team Names

To develop cohesion and spirit within a PLC, teams can create a team name that incorporates elements of the members or their goals. Team names can remain constant over the years, or the team may decide to change their name as members and instructional goals change. In this way, they keep their current concerns front and center for all to embrace.

In addition to creating a name, some groups also create a team symbol and slogan. These may seem like frivolous things for members of learning communities to do, but cooperative learning research shows that members of a group work harder to achieve the group goals when they feel emotionally connected to the group and when they feel like they can trust their team (Johnson & Johnson, 1998). In brief, it's all about team building; PLC teams can never do enough to build trust within teams. Choosing a name or creating a slogan serve that purpose well.

Action Option 2: Tear-Share

A PLC can use the Tear-Share activity to process the content of this chapter. Simply divide the group into teams of three or four. Have members number off (1, 2, 3, 4) within the teams. Then, direct each member to fold a sheet of paper in half vertically and horizontally to create four sections. They should number the sections, and write the four questions that follow in the appropriate squares (see fig. 5.1, page 98). (See page 100 for a reproducible of this activity. Visit **go.solution-tree.com/instruction** to download all reproducibles in this book.)

Each member of the group then writes his or her answers to the questions and tears the paper into four separate pieces. Once everyone in the group is done tearing, they pass the answers to the appropriate person in their group: person number one receives all of the responses to the first question, person number two receives the responses to the second question, and so on.

Each person now takes the four responses to his or her designated question on differentiation, reads them over, and prepares to present an oral summary. If there are three people in the group, the responses to question four can be set aside to be discussed by the group as a whole later.

When everyone has had a chance to read over the different answers, members share the summaries with the team as a whole. After everyone has shared, the group may discuss the content of the chapter as well as the answers to the questions.

Another option is to use the Tear-Share activity in conjunction with a journal article. The article can be read prior to the team meeting. This activity can be an efficient way to process the information in a short period of time. In this strategy, everyone reads, everyone answers each question, and then everyone shares the answers. It's a winning strategy for PLC teams and for the kids in their classrooms.

1. Describe differentiated instruction.

2. Rank the three ways teachers can differentiate process by ease of use:

    _____Changes in the model of direct instruction

    _____Changes in cooperative interactions

    _____Changes in modes of inquiry

3. Compare and contrast problem-based learning and case studies.

4. Extracurricular activities (yearbook, school newspaper, school play) should be the centerpiece of the curriculum. Do you agree or disagree? Why?

Figure 5.1: Sample tear-share differentiation box.

Action Option 3: "Turn to Your Partner and . . . "

"Turn to Your Partner and . . . " is an easy, informal partner interaction that punctuates a long talk or film (Fogarty, 2009). In this simple interaction, workshop participants are asked to talk to a partner, discussing the talk or film. In a classroom setting, teachers ask students to turn to someone near them and dialogue as partners. For example, the teacher might ask them to agree or disagree on a statement made in the lecture about personal rights. It is a quick and easy pairing for a fast dialogue between the two people to anchor the learning. Also, pairs make a great team for preparing a presentation or working in a debate mode.

Action Option 4: Think-Pair-Share

Think-Pair-Share is a similar, yet more structured partner strategy to use in PLC team sessions to get everyone talking. First, the facilitator asks individuals to think on their own about a specific concept, such as *differentiation*; then the facilitator directs them to talk about their ideas in pairs; and finally, the facilitator asks them to present a shared opinion, having reached some agreement. An example of Think-Pair-Share in the classroom might involve reviewing math word problems. Pairs do the problem individually and then talk with their partners about the solution. Finally, the pair comes to a shared response that both partners agree to.

Action Option 5: The Three Musketeers

The Three Musketeers is a cooperative group strategy that consists of a random gathering of three team members who meet to share ideas about a topic targeted by the PLC team facilitator. For example, the focus might be on homework strategies that work. In the three-way discussion, teachers talk about techniques they have discovered and used successfully. Team members find two other partners, whom they do not work with regularly, by putting one hand in the air and walking around until three of them form a teepee with their outstretched hands. Once in their groups, they may simply take turns sharing, or they may number off in their threesomes and take turns responding to specific facilitator-directed prompts. This activity works well in classrooms as well and can be easily adjusted to the topic at hand. The Three Musketeers are called the Three Cyberteers when the teacher or student discussions focus on technology-oriented topics or skills.

Tear-Share Differentiation Box

1. Describe differentiated instruction.

2. Rank the three ways teachers can differentiate process by ease of use:

   ____Changes in the model of direct instruction

   ____Changes in cooperative interactions

   ____Changes in modes of inquiry

3. Compare and contrast problem-based learning and case studies.

4. Extracurricular activities (yearbook, school newspaper, school play) should be the centerpiece of the curriculum. Do you agree or disagree? Why?

CHAPTER 6

CHANGING THE PRODUCT

PLC TAKE AWAY

Learning How Teachers Differentiate Product Options to
Meet Student Needs

Chapter 6 examines several elements that help PLC teams determine what students know and how well they know it through product differentiation. Products or performances represent the outcome or evidence of learning; these are the visible, tangible, actual end points that indicate what students know and are able to do. Products can be differentiated in both quality of work and substance. When teachers differentiate by changing the product, when they foster challenge and choice in acceptable end products, they are practicing differentiation in authentic ways.

This chapter explores how PLC teams can support the various strengths of students by welcoming different types of end products. We then present strategies for developing and accepting differing entry points to the learning, based on the work of Gardner (1999) and the highly credible, layman's version of the multiple intelligences by Armstrong (1999). These sources provide countless viable, creative options that address the many talents and needs of students served by the professional learning communities. Next, we explore the resulting exit points and describe a spectrum of expressive modes that are acceptable measures for students to demonstrate evidence of their learning. We discuss issues of accountability and how PLCs adapt a balanced assessment system that includes traditional measures of tests and quizzes, as well as common assessments, student portfolios, and student performances guided by established scoring rubrics. Finally, we include examples of changing the product for all grade levels, and of course, the chapter ends with Action Options for PLC teams to use as they unpack this idea of differentiating the product.

Three Approaches to Changing the Product

The three approaches to changing the product begin with *differentiating the entry points* to learning—giving students different ways to enter into the learning. Interestingly, the entry point of the teaching-learning process often determines how those students present evidence of that learning. When students choose to write a research report rather than make a PowerPoint presentation, or to deliver a speech rather than conduct surveys and interviews, they are already determining the shape, size, and sound of their products.

The second method of changing the product is in *differentiating the exit point*. As stated previously, this expression is in some ways determined by the entry point, yet the actual execution of the final product has multiple dimensions that provide opportunity for student choice and challenge. By generating many acceptable options for student products, PLC teams support the differentiated classroom and take another step toward ensuring student success. Students can exhibit their best work, their best evidence of learning, through designing and producing demonstrations of learning around their strengths. For example, when a student writes well, he may choose a written form of evidence, and when a student draws well, he may choose a more representative type of evidence. Both products can serve as acceptable measures of the learning, and both measures can demonstrate the quality of the learning.

The third method of changing the product has to do with *accountability for student learning* and how teachers provide the rigor and flexibility that differentiated, learner-centered instruction demands. When teachers provide varying entry points to student learning and a diversity of exit points or expressions of that learning, they also have a variety of assessment options. These options range from the very traditional—point in time, work samples, graded papers, homework checklists, tests, and common assessments—to real and virtual portfolios of student work gathered over time or authentic student performances or products aligned to a scoring rubric of required criteria and quality indicators.

While it's not that complicated to think or talk about the concept of product variances, it's quite different to actually provide these product options in the classroom. The traditional thinking about this type of differentiation is exactly what the teams in the learning communities must dissect.

Teachers want and need a repertoire of assessment strategies in order to judge the quantity and quality of student effort and student knowledge. PLCs provide the culture to create rich banks of ideas for both formative and summative assessments of the learning. Using routine, reflective, and rigorous assessments, PLCs can differentiate both the product and the accountability measures quite handily. After all, the focus in PLCs is often on assessment and accountability, and that is no different in the differentiated classroom.

Changing the Entry Points

Changing the entry points to the learning involves changing the modality of the learning. Modalities are different modes or methods of learning that provide varying ways to approach the lesson, thus setting a path for possible or probable ways to exit the learning. It seems a bit confusing at first as PLCs think about all the different ways students can learn about a lesson topic or unit of study. Yet as the teams continue to value student learning profiles, the concept of learning styles, and the spectrum of intelligences that Gardner (1999) has identified as present in every learner, the teachers embrace the idea of many doorways to learning, all leading to outcomes that meet or exceed the standards. Thus, entry points become an important focus of lesson design and unit planning for teams working within a PLC supporting differentiated instruction.

A manageable way to look at modalities or learning modes is through the eight multiple intelligences that Gardner (1999) identified as ways of producing ideas and problem solving others, as discussed in chapter 3:

1. Verbal/linguistic
2. Visual/spatial
3. Interpersonal/social
4. Intrapersonal/self
5. Mathematical/logical
6. Musical/rhythmic
7. Naturalist/physical world
8. Bodily/kinesthetic

While the research on the intelligences is sometimes questioned, educators readily acknowledge that the concept of various types of minds serves the instructional repertoire of the classroom teacher.

This practical framework of intelligences, based on Gardner's (1983) study of prodigies in the field, hypothesizes that if there are those rich with a proclivity, then, possibly, all human beings have that same intelligence at some level. According to the theory, each of us has a jagged profile of these intelligences that is as unique as our fingerprints. Thus, using this idea of a profile of talents, or multiple intelligences, serves the teacher as a ready tool for differentiating an entry point.

These intelligences were identified and introduced to the psychological and educational communities in Gardner's (1983) seminal book *Frames of Mind*. While these multiple intelligences appear in chapter 3 in the discussion on learning profiles, in this chapter, we define and describe each of the eight intelligences briefly in terms of lesson design and unit planning. This recap is intended to provide common ground and shared understandings of these modalities as a planning framework for the members of the learning community. These intelligences present a clear starting line for developing a range of entry points for diverse learners. Viewing the modalities under one umbrella may make it easier for the PLC teams to manage.

In the following feature boxes, we've brainstormed listings of word associations, planning ideas, and learning activities to focus on the various modalities and help PLC teachers remember these various intelligences in an organic way. We list them in a particular order to create the mnemonic device of *VIM N B*, a take on vim 'n' vigor. It is a way to cue the eight intelligences and is a form of chunking that provides a memory prompt. Within the PLCs, teams may generate more of their own ideas, connections, and strategies for each of the eight categories. The bank of ideas becomes an ongoing process that can even be maintained on a designated website for the PLC teams. The end result is to have a wealth of strategies to consider as differentiated instruction is implemented.

Verbal/Linguistic Intelligence

Reading, writing, speaking, listening, reporting, summarizing, booklets, poems, novels, short stories, essays, newspapers, blogs, Twitter, texting, email, word processing, folktales, tall tales, fairy tales, picture books, text books, supplementary texts, magazines, journals, speeches, debates, monologues, recordings, memoirs, biographies, autobiographies, science fiction, historical fiction, nonfiction

Visual/Spatial Intelligence

Cartoons, images, comics, graphic organizers (webs, Venn diagrams, maps, charts), DVDs, videos, film, online streaming, YouTube, Hulu, TeacherTube, PD 360, PowerPoint, CAD/CAM, sketches, drafting, scale drawings, diagrams, illustrations, paintings, homemade movies, photographs, pictures, visual media, scenes, stage sets, mental images, tables, graphs, lithographs, icons, symbols

Interpersonal/Social Intelligence

Pairs, partners, buddies, small groups, teams, social skills, roles and responsibilities, trios, duos, dialogues, articulations, conversations, discussions, debriefings, sharing, comparing, team building, collaborations, debates, arguments, points of view, AB pairs, taking turns, round-robin, back and forth, peer work, peer edits, peer tutors, peer assessments, lab partners, quads

Intrapersonal/Self Intelligence

Self-awareness, self-reflection, self-assessment, introspection, journals, diaries, learning logs, reflective dialogues, mindfulness, Habits of Mind (persisting, persevering, decreasing impulsivity, wonderment, accuracy, precision), tolerance for ambiguity, leadership, team player, goals, goal setting, self-appraisal, self-monitoring, self-starter, self-control, attitude, dispositions, demeanor

Mathematical/Logical Intelligence

Mathematics, counting, numeracy, geometry, algebra, equations, formula, calculus, problem solving, logic, logical thinking, logical argument, logical discourse, logical persuasion, reasoning, inductive and deductive thinking, calculations, computations, adding, subtracting, multiplying, dividing, statistics, statistical logic, cause and effect, conclusions, inferences

Musical/Rhythmic Intelligence

Musical beat, rhythm, melody, tune, tuning fork, harmony, symphony, performance, appreciation, orchestra, background music, elevator music, jazz, blues, rock and roll, rap, lyrics, strings, horns, percussions, solo, quartet, band, violin, cello, harp, clarinet, bugle, trumpet, trombone, bass, guitar, banjo, symbols, songs, song writers, lyricists, producers, recordings, iPod, playlist

Naturalist/Physical World Intelligence

Classification, hierarchy, sort, group, cluster, flora and fauna, surroundings, environment, jungle, concrete jungle, prairie, mountains, field walks, field trips, excursions, bird-watching, observations, zoos, farms, beehives, gardens, garden walks, aquariums, planetariums, earth science, astronomy, telescopes, microscopes, climate, weather, solar and lunar studies

> ### Bodily/Kinesthetic Intelligence
>
> Hands-on, manipulatives, labs, experiments, tools, building, models, diora-mas, scale models, doing, acting, role-playing, exercising, manipulating, moving, constructing, taking apart, putting together, repairing, improving, fixing, experiencing, field trips, excursions, guest speakers, touching, tactile, being there, becoming the thing, managing the environment, senses

These intelligences inform teachers about the talents of individual students. In the process of developing learner profiles by observing how students interact with the learning environment, teachers gather clues as to which entry points work best for particular students. Armed with this information and an enriched learning environment of many choices, teachers can direct students toward accessible entry points to help them learn more easily (Fogarty & Stoehr, 2008).

When students know how they learn best, they can make informed choices about their entry points to learning. Between the teacher's understanding and the student's awareness of the multiple intelligences or multimodal approach, learning can be tailored for optimal student achievement. For example, if a student is good with her hands, a bodily approach to learning geographical information might work well. This student might create a relief map and incorporate relevant details of her learning into the model. In another scenario, the learner may be very logical and mathematical in his thinking and prefer to learn about the geographical region through a computer software program. Still another student, who seems to learn best in a visual mode, may choose to create an illustration to display her understanding of the geography.

Knowledge and acceptance of these varied intelligences provide a ready checklist of modalities that teachers use in planning rich, relevant, and rigorous learning options. This is, in fact, some of the most effective work of PLCs. The teachers come together and plan, revise, and re-revise, until they know they have learning options with entry points for all types of learners.

The deliberate focus on how students learn causes teachers to stretch their thinking to provide a more robust approach for students. For example, they may have specific and varied readings for those who excel in the verbal intelligence, or they may provide a partner reading along with an audiotape or recording for others to glean key information. While one student may choose to create an original song—a musical product—to share what he or she has learned, another may choose to create an artistic collage—a visual and bodily product—to share similar information in an entirely different way. By providing these varied entry points to learning, teachers are, in essence, providing pathways to certain genres of end products as well.

Offering different entry points doesn't mean that teachers must offer eight learning options for every lesson or that all eight intelligences must be a part of every lesson. It simply means that learners need some options in how they go about their learning. Thus, when teachers design the learning situations, they should plan for two or more possible entry points.

Teachers involved in the culture and spirit of PLCs soon learn and often agree, after working with these eight intelligences, that it is next to impossible for quality teaching to occur without engaging a number of modalities. The student who uses a hands-on approach could simultaneously use an interpersonal or a musical approach. The logical mathematical learner might use the intrapersonal as well as the visual arena, as he works at the computer. In turn, the visual learner could combine the bodily intelligence with the naturalist intelligence as he represents his learning pictorially as a mural.

The concept of different entry points to learning becomes quite manageable for the teachers in PLCs when they collaborate on lessons or units for differentiated classroom instruction. Diverse learners welcome options for learning that allow them to exhibit their talents in myriad ways. Changing entry points by encompassing a range of modalities, intelligences, and styles in lesson design and unit planning is a powerful task for PLCs to pursue.

Please note that the chapter ends with elementary, middle, and high school examples of changing the product by changing the entry points (page 115).

Changing the Exit Points

Just as learners have propensities for entering learning through different doors, they may also exhibit preferences for expressing their learning in different ways. To change the exit points for expressing what one knows and is able to do, teachers can again use the spectrum of intelligences as a framework. It's natural for students to move to the modality or combination of modalities that they are most comfortable with. They seek the mode that they feel confident about and the intelligences they know they handle well.

When teachers plan for the outcomes of the learning, whether it be in a robust lesson or in a rigorous unit of study, they may require some exit point for students to exhibit evidence of their individual learning. These expressions of their knowledge base and the concepts and skills they have learned manifest themselves in the student-generated products or student performances.

By letting students select from a list of options, and choose the expressive mode or modes they prefer, teachers differentiate a major part of the learning curve. When students choose an option to show what they have learned, they begin a critical part of the learning as they put the project or performance together. To plan, organize, and execute their selected options is learning at its best.

Based on the same eight modalities of Gardner's multiple intelligences (1999), Armstrong's (1999) work represents them in practical terms that appeal to students. Armstrong writes about the different kinds of "smart" in his listings. In the list that follows are Armstrong's terms for the various kinds of smarts one has. We have also included our own short, pithy sayings to denote the meanings of these kinds of smarts:

- Word smart—The person doing the talking is the person doing the learning.
- Logic smart—What's counted counts!
- Art smart—I must see it before I can say it.
- Nature smart—Nature reigns supreme.
- Self smart—Intelligence is knowing what you know and don't know.
- People smart—The world is social, and I am part of it.
- Music smart—Music is the universal language.
- Body smart—Just do it.

These sayings are kid-friendly ways for students to think about their learning profiles and their learning styles. Teachers guide the exit point decisions as students appraise their own strengths and weaknesses. And, just as it has been throughout the discussion, teachers working in PLCs provide the needed brainstorms and collegial conversations to create a bank of ideas to offer as student choices.

For example, if students are logic smart, as Armstrong (1999) labels it, let them express themselves electronically using logical, deductive reasoning to navigate complex computer software. If students are art smart, let them depict their artistic thinking through one of the visual arts. If they are nature smart, let them tap into environmental learning and assessments. If they are people smart, let them lead the teams in learning investigations and explorations and organize group presentations of their findings. If students are self smart, lead them toward introspective kinds of learning and evaluation tools. If they are music smart, encourage them to use the media of music to express their understandings. If they are body smart, let them express their learning through dance, drama, mime, and puppetry.

Since the eight modalities have been discussed in depth multiple times, their importance in differentiating curriculum and instruction is obvious. There is no way to truly offer options to students for entry points and exit points without tapping into these various realms. In fact, the idea that these intelligences guide the teaching and learning equation is something that teams immersed in PLCs come to appreciate and willingly address. They know that the more choices and challenges they can offer to each and every student—and the more changes they can offer in the content, processes, and products—the more advantages students have to demonstrate their success.

In short, when teachers let students determine how they could best demonstrate what they know about a particular topic and how they can apply that learning in relevant ways, students will execute that challenge more successfully. When students think about how to best display their understanding and demonstrate evidence of their personal learning, differentiation is working. When students make maps, build models, invent contraptions, demonstrate chemical reactions, design posters, create plays, simulate a historical event, write their own autobiographies, read to senior citizens, follow a current event with a personal blog, or otherwise show what they know in incredibly creative ways, then the learning communities can celebrate their progress with differentiated instruction.

Please note that the chapter ends with elementary, middle, and high school examples of changing the product by changing the expressive modes.

Changing the Methods of Accountability

Assessment is the companion of changing the product. To assess products is to hold students accountable for their choice of how they show their evidence of learning. The assessment judges not only the quantity of that learning, but also the quality.

It's important to note that when teachers differentiate learning by changing the accountability factor, that does not mean students are not responsible for the learning. It means that teachers in the PLC teams provide different ways for students to be accountable for the learning. To vary the accountability measures whenever possible and to look for a robust picture of student learning, teachers use summative and formative assessments as well as a balanced assessment plan that includes traditional, verbal/linguistic assessments; portfolios of artifacts and reflections; and performance data with predetermined criteria and quality indicators. A brief description of these many elements follows.

Summative Assessments

In traditional classrooms, summative assessments are the most common form of judgment on student-produced evidence of learning. This is the case in differentiated instruction classrooms as well. Teachers in PLCs need final feedback—a summative assessment—on student progress, skills, and concepts. Summative assessments evaluate the evidence of learning by way of student products and performances; standardized, end-of-course or end-of-chapter test data; and data gleaned from scoring rubrics, class work, or even homework. A more complete list of summative assessment types includes the following:

- Norm-referenced tests
- Standardized tests
- Criterion-referenced tests
- End-of-course tests
- Chapter tests
- Weekly quizzes

Summative assessments of student work often translate into grades and rankings. They provide the hard data used to make placement decisions, though they are sometimes used in more formative ways, for example, to prompt recommendations for flexible skills groupings. At the end of the day, however, summative assessments are just that: a summation of the students' work. Summative achievement data from the previous school year provide valued information as an early screening device to assess what students know and don't know in terms of concepts and skills at the beginning of the next school year. They give teacher teams working within PLCs a long look at the entire achievement profile of their group as well as individual students. Through checklists and scoring rubrics, students are held accountable for their chosen products or performances. Summative data are wanted and warranted by PLCs as part of their ongoing evaluation of students.

Formative Assessments

Summative assessments are not the only accountability measure that matters, however. In fact, formative assessments, classroom assessment *for* learning, play significant roles in the entire teaching-and-learning process. Formative assessments allow teachers and students to "form" opinions along the learning journey about best next steps. Teams should integrate formative assessments into the actual instruction to better inform instructional practice. These measures signal teachers and students that things are going well or alert teachers that students are getting lost, are not understanding, or are unable able to do the skill as practiced.

Formative assessments inform teachers and students in the moment, when there is time and opportunity to adjust instruction to ensure success for all students (Fogarty & Kerns, 2009). Following is a breakdown of these tactics:

- Routine—every day, all day
  - ✚ Agree-disagree strategy
  - ✚ Signaling

- ✦ Questioning
- ✦ Pop quizzes
- ● Reflective—many days
  - ✦ Peer dialogues
  - ✦ Journals
  - ✦ Question-and-answer sessions
  - ✦ Metacognitive self-monitoring
- ● Rigorous—some days
  - ✦ Examination of student work
  - ✦ Analysis of tests
  - ✦ Test-development software
  - ✦ Common assessments

In the differentiated classrooms supported by PLCs, formative assessment measures are valued greatly for the information they reveal. Formative assessments are the nuts and bolts of differentiated instruction because they provide the needed feedback for teachers and students to act upon. Teachers and students confer regularly to track progress and to ensure understanding and accuracy of the tasks involved. There is two-way communication when students engage in projects. In addition, collaborative conversations and moments of reflection are woven into PLC team meetings.

Balanced Assessment Plan

In addition to using a combination of formative and summative assessments, teachers should use a balance of assessment methods (Fogarty, 1999) that include traditional measures, portfolios of work, and authentic performances. In this way, students have ample opportunities to depict the evidence of their learning. Each of these measures provides confirmation of learning and can be used in a variety of combinations based on the kinds of products students have produced. Learning communities use these many types of assessments to determine what students know and don't know and what the next steps need to be.

Traditional Measures of Assessment

When using traditional measures such as tests, quizzes, standardized tests, and other pencil-and-paper tasks, the measurement is recorded in grades and rankings. When teams of teachers working within PLCs take on the task of writing common assessments, however, what may have been a traditional summative test model is now changed to a formative assessment model. These data, gleaned from common assessments, are important and definitely provide valuable information about student learning.

When traditional measures are used in formative ways, teachers in learning communities have the best of both worlds. They have hard data to plot where students are academically for reporting purposes, but more importantly, with disaggregated data from tests, they also have cues and clues as to where students need help. Thus, data inform their teaching. Further, when these traditional measures are changed to accommodate certain types of learners, they can provide solid feedback on the students' progress or level of understanding. Teachers talking in their PLC teams share ideas, for example, about using oral quizzes instead of written ones, providing a translation buddy for second language learners, and allowing partners to work together on a written test.

In addition, traditional accountability measures can be shifted radically to provide support and success for students. For instance, Reeves (2002) advocates (1) not giving zeros for incomplete work, instead requiring students to always finish the work; (2) not averaging, instead grading on what the student knows and takes away; and most importantly (3) not having a "killer" project that accounts for a huge percentage of the course grade, instead scaffolding the project with benchmarks along the way. Reeves's suggestions provide great fodder for learning communities to discuss as they look at ways to change the product and ensure student success.

The following accountability strategies emphasize finding out what students know, rather than punishing students unskilled in test taking (Reeves, 2002).

Student Portfolio Assessments

By incorporating student portfolios, teachers gain a different perspective on what students have learned. Portfolios provide real or virtual artifacts of learning that demonstrate growth and development. Whether on a website or in a manila folder, student portfolios enhance the information obtained from tests and other kinds of traditional grades and rankings for students, teachers, and parents.

Portfolios show works in progress or final entries; they can even show a biography of a work, with first drafts, edited versions, revisions with peer comments, and final submittals. To show development over time, portfolios can contain work from the entire term or year. Portfolios are like photo albums that speak of the many aspects of the learning process.

In fact, the portfolio is a reflective tool for self-monitoring as well. Portfolios might be simple work folders in which all work is collected, or they may be more elaborate showcase portfolios (Belgrade, Burke, & Fogarty, 2008) in which work is selected and reflected upon. And of course they can be paper or electronic. Regardless, all models contain artifacts of student work: writing, outlines, pictures, photos, and reflections. Portfolios are really *process*-folios that epitomize the culture and spirit of learning organizations.

A portfolio process involves, at minimum, three stages: collection, selection, and reflection. Students *collect* items in a working portfolio centered on a unit of study or a course term. As the unit or term approaches an end, students *select* items for the showcase portfolio. Once they have decided on these final items, students *reflect* on why they chose the items as evidence of their learning.

Portfolios of work are done with a sense of audience. That audience may be the teacher in a student-teacher conference, it may be peers in peer reviews, or it may be parents in a parent conference setting or even at home. No matter who the audience is, it is in this final step—when students revisit their portfolio products—that reflective learning occurs.

Performance Assessments

Performance assessments complete the balance of different methods of accountability. By requiring students to demonstrate what they know and are able to do, PLC teacher teams create another highly valued dimension of assessing student learning. The performance is the proof that students really understand and can apply the learning. It takes the learning from inert knowledge to concrete application. For students to know how to write a coherent piece, for example, whether it be narrative or informative in nature, they must write frequently on flexible and varied assignments in both the narrative and expository veins. When students perform those tasks often, they develop skillfulness that shows up on the tests and in the written work.

Performances include, among other things, role-plays, drama, musicals, speeches, debates, and personal and PowerPoint presentations. They can also include students giving a speech at a science fair booth, reading to a younger class, or interviewing a local celebrity. Performances are those hands-on, in-person, up-front kinds of tasks that show a student's sense of self, confidence level, and stage presence. These performances are high stakes and the students know it, so anything the PLC teams can devise to make these situations more comfortable and more successful for students serves their students well.

Of course, the performance category of assessing student learning usually carries with it a scoring rubric, or at the least a checklist of requirements that students must meet. Without getting into the whole process of developing rubrics for projects and performances, there are general guidelines that make a rubric more genuine and appropriate. Experts agree that scoring rubrics should include *criteria* such as content, presentation, and originality as well as *indicators of quality* that progress from low to high with standard statements of the quality being judged (Burke, 2009; Marzano, McTighe, & Pickering, 1997; see figure 6.1). (See page 119 for a reproducible of this rubric. Visit **go.solution-tree.com/instruction** to download all reproducibles in this book.) It is often further recommended that there be four indicators of quality rather than three or five, because it is too easy to mark the middle indicator and not distinguish the differences clearly.

Standard:				
Title of Project, Product, or Performance:				
	DEVELOPING	**COMPETENT**	**PROFICIENT**	**DISTINGUISHED**
CONTENT	Incomplete; items missing or no reflections	All components completed with reflections	Complete with insightful reflections	Complete, outstanding content and memorable reflections
APPEARANCE	No evidence of formatting or additional structures to appearance	Formatting and design elements evident	Formatting and design notable and appropriate	Remarkable design with originality and elaboration
PRESENTATION	Disorganized with little flow to the presentation	Organized and sequenced	Organized flow and expression	Organized with fluency and expression

Figure 6.1: Sample scoring rubric.

The development of the scoring rubric precedes the projects. In this way, teachers and students understand the expectations of the assignments beforehand. In addition, the rubrics are sometimes developed with the students to get even more buy-in and common understanding of the goals. While creating scoring rubrics is work that teacher teams within the PLCs often do together, once students are familiar with rubrics and their components, they can become very skillful in developing them with the teachers. At that point, the rubric truly becomes a student-centered, student-owned product of performance with built-in accountability.

Again, developing rubrics together as PLC teams is extremely productive. The conversations are invaluable as teachers explain and defend their thoughts about "acceptable" and "exceptional" quality of student work. It is well worth the time and energy to engage in the rubric development process.

To summarize, differentiated or balanced assessment models are comprised of three powerful sets of tools that provide a spectrum of information on student learning: (1) traditional assessments (tests, quizzes, works samples, and common assessments), (2) student learning portfolios (writing folders, work samples, and biography of a work), and (3) performance assessments (projects, presentations, and actual performances). In brief, when the teacher uses differentiated methods for holding students accountable, student differences are honored, resulting in a full picture of student accomplishments. The combination of the three methods provides a rich portrait of student learning and is the responsible approach to assessment.

Examples of Changing the Product

Following are examples of differentiating the product by changing the entry points, the exit points, and the method of accountability.

Elementary School Examples

Changing the entry points: *Parts of speech*

- Verbal—Use a magazine page, and circle the verbs or adjectives.
- Visual—Create a collage of the parts of speech.
- Interpersonal—Use flash cards with the parts of speech.
- Musical—Write a limerick about the parts of speech.

Changing the exit points: *Human body*

- Art smart—Draw a skeleton diagram with labels.
- People smart—In pairs, trace your partner's profile on large paper.
- Music smart—Find and learn the song "Dem Bones" ("Your neck bone's connected to . . .").

Changing the method of accountability: *Physical education*

- Traditional—Track your exercise data for a week.
- Portfolio—Collect and show evidence of the PE games and sports.
- Performance—Plan a brief gym demonstration for a younger class.

Middle School Examples

Changing the entry points: *Geography*

- Visual—Illustrate maps of a specific region.
- Mathematical—Use a computer software program.
- Bodily—Build a model relief map of a specific region.

Changing the exit points: *Novels*

- Word smart—Gather twenty new and intriguing words, and illustrate in a notebook.

- People smart—Profile one character, and compare to yourself.
- Body smart—Create a brief play of the story.

Changing the method of accountability: *Civil War*

- Traditional—Write letters to the soldiers of the Union and the Confederate armies.
- Portfolio—Create a brochure of the key events.
- Performance—Reenact the Gettysburg Address.

High School Examples

Changing the entry points: *Consumer economics*

- Verbal—Write an op-ed on the obesity challenge America faces.
- Mathematical—Conduct a supermarket survey of data.
- Naturalist—Develop a heart-healthy, brain-friendly menu for a month.

Changing the exit points: *Statistics*

- People smart—Interview an insurance agent on longevity tables and reports.
- Self smart—Create a stock portfolio of your favorite companies.
- Logic smart—Track your stock for three months.

Changing the method of accountability: *Cycles* (cross-curricular)

- Traditional—Complete a written test on the life cycle (biology).
- Portfolio—Create an electronic portfolio of current events cycles (American history).
- Performance—Debate the paradox of the end as the beginning (speech).

Action Options

PLC TAKE AWAY

Learning How Teachers Differentiate Product Options to
Meet Student Needs

Differentiation is about change, challenge, and choice. It's about student readiness, student interests, and student learning profiles. It's about challenging students to reach the high end of the learning continuum that calls for more independent work, open-ended issues to tackle, products and performances that are transformative, and ongoing formative assessments that help target their learning goals.

It should not matter how students demonstrate what they have learned. If the teaching-learning equation is successful, there can be as much variety in the proof of understanding as there can be variety in the way it is taught or learned. What does matter is that the heart of the work is the belief in continual and constant assessment techniques. Products, performances, and accountability are the lifeblood of authentic learning, and they are the measures that inform PLC teams about student success. These tools reveal what students know and don't know and produce the data that help teachers make critical instructional decisions in differentiated classroom settings.

The Action Options for this chapter include Pick Three and Plus, Minus, Interesting. Each of these exercises is intended to deepen the understanding of changing the product options to meet the talent and needs of students. These strategies are the learning side of the teaching-learning equation for the adult learners in teacher teams. Visit www.allthingsplc.info/evidence/raymoreelementaryschool/index.php to learn more about the value of teacher-designed rubrics that support differentiation.

Action Option 1: Pick Three

Here is a simple but effective way for members of the PLC to experience what it means to offer choices for a student to express what he or she has learned. Assign chapter 6 of *Supporting Differentiated Instruction* for the team to read. At the next meeting, place a piece of paper for each member of the team in a basket. On a third of the pieces of paper, write "Oral Summary"; on the next third, "Written Summary"; and on the remaining third, "Graphic Organizer." Members will choose a slip randomly, and these slips will determine how the various members will express what they have learned from chapter 6. The purpose of this drawing is to encourage members to try something different and to show the many possibilities for responding to the reading. Each presentation should include:

- Ways teachers can differentiate the product
- A reference to Gardner's theory of multiple intelligences
- A reference to Armstrong's (1999) *7 Kinds of Smart*
- Types of assessment

These requirements should be provided to members in the form of a checklist to guide the quality of their work. Each member prepares his or her summary as prescribed: written, oral, or graphic. Participants should take four to five minutes to prepare and two minutes to present.

After each person picks a piece of paper from the basket, the facilitator should divide the group into three teams—one for each type of end point—and instruct them to debrief accordingly, plan together, and then prepare their summaries together. When everyone is ready to present, the facilitator should divide the groups into new teams, each with representatives of the three types. The members will present summaries in these small teams or to the whole PLC team if it is small (three to nine people).

It is a simple jigsaw activity, yet it demonstrates to the PLC team how the product of a lesson can be changed by altering the way students prove what they have learned. While it does not change the way each participant engaged with the material, or the way they were assessed, it does change the product for assessment.

The checklist, an important tool in this activity, makes the learning goal for the PLC teachers explicit, just as teachers should do with students.

Action Option 2: Plus, Minus, Interesting

Plus, Minus, Interesting (PMI) is an effective evaluation tool that can be applied to many situations in PLCs and classrooms. In this case, team members are asked to rate the idea of traditional measures of assessment (tests, quizzes, work samples, homework, grading, grade point averages, and so on). In the group, with someone recording on a chart, members briefly discuss the pluses, the minuses, and the interesting aspects of traditional measures of assessment. For example, for *homework*, the plus might be that it allows students to revisit the day's work; a minus might be that, at times, there is no one to help students with homework; and an interesting aspect might be that homework is controversial, with lots of articles breaking down the debate. The PMI activity usually results in a lively discussion.

Sample Scoring Rubric

Standard:

Title of Project, Product, or Performance:

	DEVELOPING	COMPETENT	PROFICIENT	DISTINGUISHED
CONTENT	Incomplete; items missing or no reflections	All components completed with reflections	Complete with insightful reflections	Complete, outstanding content and memorable reflections
APPEARANCE	No evidence of formatting or additional structures to appearance	Formatting and design elements evident	Formatting and design notable and appropriate	Remarkable design with originality and elaboration
PRESENTATION	Disorganized with little flow to the presentation	Organized and sequenced	Organized flow and expression	Organized with fluency and expression

CHAPTER **7**

DIVERSE-LEARNER STRATEGIES

PLC TAKE AWAY

Learning How PLCs Share Differentiation Strategies for
Diverse Learners

We now circle back to a focus on learners by giving teachers within professional learning communities another way to appraise their students. Unlike the earlier chapters in which methods for identifying individual learner needs were addressed, this chapter looks at typical learner archetypes that comprise the diversity of today's K–12 classrooms.

While differentiated instruction sometimes targets individuals, much of the time teachers plan instruction for various categories of learners. In short, they are not planning a different lesson for each student, but instead are planning lessons with differentiated strategies that ensure all student needs are met. This chapter develops a summary look at different kinds of learners—developing learners, advanced learners, English learners, and learners with special needs—through archetypes in children's literature. We've included lists of strategies commonly used to address the talents and needs of these various archetypes for teacher teams to explore.

As teachers read about this compendium of strategies for the various learner archetypes, they should add their own ideas to the list. Note that, as in every chapter, we've provided Action Options for teams to try as they support differentiated instruction in their schools.

Finally, the discussion returns to the centerpiece of differentiated instruction: a diverse and varied student body. While chapter 3 focuses on identifying individual students' readiness levels, personal interests, and learning profiles, this discussion captures the learner talents and needs through an elaboration of the four learner archetypes.

Developing Learners

Developing and struggling learners must remain a focal point for differentiated instruction. In many cases, and for as many reasons, these learners may have developmental lags. They may have started school at a younger age than others, moved frequently during and throughout their schooling years, or be children from poverty with deficiencies in their background knowledge and life experiences.

As a result, these developing learners may struggle to keep up in some or all subjects. Many of these students are missing critical skills in literacy and math that would have prepared them for the current curriculum content; they have noticeable gaps in learning that truly interrupt their abilities—and impair their readiness—to learn new material. Such students exhibit little prior knowledge to ground new learning with relevant connections, and they need instructional interventions.

Immediate, specific, and consistent attention through differentiated approaches to instruction can help these students. In many cases, teachers already have differentiated learning strategies for developing and struggling learners, which is the perfect starting point for learning communities. They can focus their collaborative conversations on the existing tools and techniques that they already use with students in need.

To facilitate the discussion, PLC teams may benefit from a visual image as a conversation catalyst. To that end, *Leo the Late Bloomer* (Krause, 1971) is profiled here. The lead character, Leo, is an archetype of the developing learner, struggling to catch up. In the story, readers get to know Leo quite well. Leo can't read. He is, in fact, fairly nonverbal; he is obviously a slow-developing youngster, yet he seems happy and does not exhibit any signs of anxiety about not doing what other kids are doing. Instead, Leo is adventurous, curious, nature loving, and eager to learn.

From the education perspective, however, Leo, who is just beginning school, can't seem to do anything right. He doesn't read, write, or even draw. His mom says that he's just a late bloomer. Everyone watches and tries to help Leo, to see if he shows signs of blooming. Finally, with all the watching and all the trying, something magical happens. Leo does indeed bloom, and he is on his way toward a more successful and satisfying school experience.

Now, of course this is just a children's book, but it gives the learning communities common ground for generating a list of strategies for developing or struggling learners. This collaboration is a prime example of what Schmoker (1996) talks about in his work on school improvement. Through the conversations that occur, teachers dig into their own experiences and are surprised at how much they know and do to ensure success for these developing learners struggling to keep up.

Among the many ideas that PLC teams share, the following strategies are sure to appear on the list:

- Identify and close learning gaps.
- Structure activities.
- Use concrete activities.
- Use fewer steps.
- Use activities similar or close to the desired behavior.
- Assign simpler reading.
- Create a deliberate pace.
- Monitor constantly.

Effective teachers identify the learning gaps and find ways to fill those gaps with one-to-one interventions or flexible skill groupings. They use more direct instruction and more scaffolding or step-by-step instruction with these kids. They also provide more structured activities with fewer and clearer steps to recall.

Teachers working with developing or struggling learners can share how they use more concrete, hands-on learning that is close to the actual desired performance for the student. The best illustration of this concept is learning to drive in a simulator before getting in the real car on the real road. For example, teachers might orchestrate an experiment that allows students to feel the swing of the pendulum to develop the concept of motion, rather than simply tell them about it. Or perhaps students practice adverbs by writing adverbial phrases rather than a drill-and-skill activity using adverbs in isolation. Learning adverbs through adverbial phrases is closer to what they will encounter in writing, unlike rote memorization. Finally, they talk about the absolute necessity to use less-complex reading material and to work with routine, predictable procedures at a deliberate and monitored pace.

While this is not a complete list of strategies for developing or struggling learners, it certainly includes approaches that PLC teams can recommend and encourage. When applied consistently by entire teams of teachers, these strategies have significant impact on student success. As the teachers within PLC teams continue their work, the list grows and more strategies surface for teachers to share and apply.

Advanced Learners

At the other end of the instructional spectrum are the advanced or gifted learners. This group often comes to school with rich backgrounds, highly supportive and involved parents, and a wealth of outside resources to enhance their natural interests, inclinations, and aptitudes. However, some students who exhibit notable talent or achievement levels come to school lacking that home environment support; their gifts are recognized and advanced entirely by the school programs. Still others are not identified as talented and gifted either at home or at school; they are just considered uninterested, uninvolved, or troublemakers.

This category of students represents those who may be above average in terms of general intellectual capabilities or who have extraordinary aptitude in a particular area. The work is easy for them, and they move through coursework with speed and ease. They are often star students, excelling in many areas, who are considered very good at the game of school. Yet, as alluded to earlier, these advanced learners can also be underachieving students who are bored in their classes, academically under-challenged by the work, and who sometimes exhibit negative behaviors as a result.

In terms of gifted education, the Elementary and Secondary Education Act proposed the following areas of general high intellect: achievement in a specific academic area, usually math or language; extraordinary talent in art, music, or drama; unusual creativity; and leadership potential (National Council of Gifted Education, 2008). However, as the actual implementation of these identification processes unfold, most states choose to focus on the first two categories. The other areas are often too elusive to identify clearly so they are not usually included in the screening.

Accommodations in programming for gifted and advanced learners usually fall into two camps: (1) pull-out programs or (2) accelerated Advanced Placement (AP) courses. Elementary schools use the pull-out programs more often than acceleration, while high schools use AP courses almost exclusively for their advanced learners. Occasionally, schools sponsor early promotions to the next grade, tutorials for a talented youngster, or even apprenticeships in the field of interest. These are the early attempts at differentiating instruction for advanced learners.

PLC teams have a keen opportunity to talk about the things they have found helpful when addressing the needs of the advanced learner. Teams share their tricks of the trade in collaborative conversations, and members walk away with new ideas and approaches that they can add to their teaching repertoires.

In *Wilfrid Gordon McDonald Partridge* (Fox, 1985), the lead character is an advanced-learner archetype. Wilfrid has a friend in the nursing home next door to his house. While he knows all of the residents of the senior center, Miss Nancy Alison Delacourt Cooper is his favorite because she has four names like he does. One day, he hears his parents talking about how Miss Nancy has lost her memory. As he sets out to figure out what a memory is and how to help her find it, he asks everyone to tell him their definition of a *memory*. Based on their thoughts that a memory is something warm, sad, and cherished, he gathers objects that represent these descriptions. Finally, he has a wonderful chat with Miss Nancy, and she shares all kinds of marvelous memories with him. It is an endearing tale that provides an inspiring starting point for PLC conversations.

Wilfrid exhibits many of the traits associated with gifted or advanced learners. He is inquisitive, highly verbal, creative, resourceful, and has a knack for problem solving. He is very sociable with notable interpersonal skills, and he loves being with his friends at the senior center. Wilfrid provides the perfect archetype of the advanced learner for PLC teams to consider in their listings of appropriate and workable strategies for gifted and talented students. Some of those strategies include the following:

- Skip practice of mastered material.
- Compact information.
- Make activities complex.
- Use open-ended activities.
- Use abstract activities.
- Make activities multifaceted.
- Assign advanced reading.
- Enroll students in AP courses.
- Create activities with depth.

When working with an advanced or gifted learner, many teachers allow those students to skip the practice of mastered material and go on to the next steps, though they admit this strategy is sometimes hard to implement in a class of twenty-five students. They also talk about compacting the information so it is managed appropriately for those who are already proficient.

Teachers also add more-complex activities that require planning and organization by the student and are multifaceted and open-ended in their problem scenarios and solutions. Teams talk about advanced reading tasks that provide a depth and breadth to the learning; they consider problems that foster genuine inquiry and robust investigations and have lengthy discussions about the pros and cons of real and virtual AP courses. In addition, they discuss how easy it is to forget that these students need constant and continual challenge to be fully engaged in learning. These conversations reveal many strategies, and more importantly, they remind the PLC teams of the need for this compendium of tactics to serve that population of students.

English Learners

A third archetype present in classrooms across North America is the huge English learner (EL) demographic. Coming to school from a wide range of countries and regions, these learners include speakers of all types of languages. The task of reaching them may seem monumental when teachers first look at the percentage of students whose first language is not English, who come from different cultural backgrounds, or who are deficient in the primary language of the classroom.

The teams of teachers may spend some time talking about what these students face day in and day out as they strive to translate and interpret what is being said and what is going on in the lesson. They may also discuss the extremely high motivation these youngsters show to learn English, to learn about their new surroundings, and to belong. At the same time, discussions should include acknowledgment and acceptance of what PLC teams can do to respect and retain the integrity of the native cultures (Hispanic, African American, Maori, Singapore) their students represent. Cultural identity is a huge and complex issue in many districts and schools, and PLCs address it through implementation of their differentiated instructional plans.

The EL archetype can be seen clearly in Bishop and Wiese's (1938) tale *The Five Chinese Brothers*. In this story, there are five Chinese brothers who all look just alike. While none of them speak English, each has a special talent in the bodily/kinesthetic intelligence, such as stretching tall, holding his breath, or demonstrating a neck as strong as iron. They also exhibit keen visual intelligences and are willing, earnest, and industrious learners. One day, they all use their special talents—rather than language—to try a save a young boy who has wandered out to sea. While this is a tale of extraordinary talent, *The Five Chinese Brothers* also illustrates how students have aptitudes and propensities other than language. EL students often love the adventure that challenges present and exhibit ingenuity in their problem-solving approaches. This story serves as an excellent conversation starter for PLC teams on this subject.

Following is a list of strategies to use with EL students:

- Assign a cooperative buddy.
- Assign a translation partner.
- Use visuals such as pictures and videos as well as graphic organizers.

- Require drawings to bridge language gaps.

- Accompany visuals with auditory cues.

- Create hands-on, bodily/kinesthetic activities.

- Use activities and programs online.

EL strategies discussed in PLC teams often include partnering with a cooperative buddy for support and coaching or with a translation partner for language guidance. In addition, teachers use many visuals and graphic representations to enhance the lesson for English learners. Requiring drawing and pictures for these learners instead of written language assignments helps temporarily bridge learning. Use of visuals accompanied by auditory cues, tapes, and videos created by partners also helps students constantly hear the sound of the English language with its syntax in place, phrasing clearly articulated, and intonations audibly recorded.

PLC teams should also discuss the need for ELs to experience the learning firsthand, which is possible by including bodily/kinesthetic learning experiences. This kind of activity involves online and Web-based learning tools that require kids to use their hands-on keyboarding skills. Most teachers agree that these virtual tools have high stimuli and high motivation for English learners due to visuals, audio, and feedback for self-correction.

PLC teams can use the initial brainstormed list as a starting point and can continue to add to it as ideas occur. Over time, these strategies become second nature to teachers differentiating instruction for their English learners.

Learners With Special Needs

The archetype of learners with special needs is a broad and highly diverse category. These learners, more often than not, require direct attention or special assistance from aides. As teachers discuss these students and their talents and needs, they may reference the Individuals With Disabilities Act (1990), which dictates a student's right to work in the least restrictive environment.

Students who are eligible for special education manifest a large array of symptoms and diagnoses. For the sake of this discussion, the category of special needs is defined as students with the following diagnoses:

- Dyslexia

- Autism spectrum disorder

- Attention deficit disorder

- Attention deficit hyperactivity disorder

- Learning challenged (formerly learning disabled)

- Behaviorally challenged (formerly behavior disorder)
- Intellectually challenged (formerly mentally disabled)
- Physically challenged (hearing loss, blindness, mobility challenged, and so on)
- Social/emotional disorder

While this appears to be an overwhelming list, teacher teams in the PLC environment address these students just as they address all students. They know that they need to get to know these students well if they are to accommodate and modify learning for them in their differentiated classrooms.

Maria Shriver's *What's Wrong With Timmy* (2001) provides a compelling story of a little boy who is intellectually challenged. A girl notices Timmy on the playground and asks her mom what's wrong with him, because it seems that something is different about him. Timmy loves basketball, but feels left out, ridiculed, and not liked by the other kids. This little girl, however, befriends him and starts to play basketball with him. Eventually her friends join the game. Through this experience, she begins to understand that everyone is different, and those overcoming severe challenges have much to offer.

Timmy shows some of the traits learners with special needs may exhibit as they try to integrate, socialize, and learn with their peers. He is excited about the things he can do, motivated to do them, and eager for recognition and acknowledgment of his successes. At the same time, however, Timmy is lonely; he is aware that he is not a part of the group and longs to be invited to play with and be accepted by his peers. He responds to kindness and attention and has the unwavering support of his family and friends.

While the profile of the student's needs and his or her individual education plan (IEP) determine the exact prescription of strategies, PLC teams can produce a general, helpful list of resources:

- Classroom aide
- Tutor
- Peer partner
- Peer tutor
- Special services
- Resource teachers
- Technology tools
- Student monitoring

- Furniture and facilities modifications
- Parent involvement

Strategies for students with special needs usually begin with an IEP that spells out a curriculum plan for the student. In addition, strategies that may complement the IEP include a classroom aide to accompany the student as a constant companion and tutors or peer partners to provide ongoing support and coaching in the classroom. Specialists and resource teachers provide support and coaching outside the classroom. Technological tools are also effective alternatives for students with special needs, providing constant and immediate feedback for student monitoring. Room arrangement, environmental or limited stimuli, customized furniture, and facilities modifications are also helpful when working with learners with special needs. Finally, the genuine and consistent involvement of parents is a must in working effectively with these students. Teachers should share facilitation techniques in PLC team meetings to help build the group repertoire as well.

Differentiated instruction for learners with special needs runs the gamut from high touch to high technology. In the end, as these students respond to the changes teachers make to accommodate them, the effects are noted and the cycle of improvement continues.

It is important to note that the four profiles of learning archetypes provide information needed for the ensuing discussions. As readers turn their attention to lesson design and units of study, they utilize these archetypes to tweak the basic lesson and to plot differentiated paths of study for different types of learners. These are simple exercises in differentiation that allow teacher teams to think about and fine-tune their existing lessons. At the same time, they begin to write new differentiated lesson plans and curriculum units.

Action Options

PLC TAKE AWAY

Learning How PLCs Share Differentiation Strategies for
Diverse Learners

In the ongoing team discussions, members often discover that many of their regularly used strategies align with research (Tomlinson, 1999a). These are powerful affirmations of the skill and knowledge of these dedicated classroom teachers. Affirmation that developing learners need step-by-step scaffolding or that advanced learners benefit by skipping what they already know are examples of team wisdom. In fact, these collegial conversations are a major attribute of high-functioning learning communities, because they embrace one another as they become fellow learners. Teachers in PLCs are continually learning valued skills from one another and discovering the many positive gifts within themselves. They are the epitome of a learning organization.

Following are several Action Options about learner archetypes that bring the entire discussion back to a clear focus on learners. These Action Options include video clips that share ideas about learner types, a list of children's book characters that serve as metaphors for learners, and a marvelous activity called On a Scale of One to Ten that fosters sound self-appraisals of the teachers in the PLC teams. In addition, visit www.allthingsplc.info/pdf/articles/MakingaDifferenceOneChildataTime .pdf to read about making a difference one child at a time.

Action Option 1: Videos

Videos are a powerful debriefing tool for PLCs on the talents and needs of students, and how the teacher accommodates these students through differentiated instruction. The characters and circumstances present real issues, yet the situations allow open, bias-free discussion among PLC team members because the subjects are not real teachers or real kids.

Following are suggested films for powerful half-day or full-day sessions. We've noted specific scenes for opening or closing a PLC team session. The discussions sparked often lead to new insights about working with students.

Developing learners: *Mr. Holland's Opus* (Herek & Duncan, 1995)

Chess game on porch—Mr. Holland is challenged by his colleague to teach a student to bang a drum so the student can stay on the wrestling team. The scene shows this teacher trying many multimodal learning strategies culminating in a successful student performance on the day of the parade.

Advanced learners: *Akeelah and the Bee* (Atchison, 2006)

Jumping rope in driveway—Akeelah is practicing for the spelling bee in the driveway when her coach notices that she is using the musical rhythm and beat to help her spell the words. He gives her a jump rope to use as she continues to practice with this musical memory device.

English learners: *Freedom Writers* (LaGravenese, 2007)

Celebration party—The high school writing teacher has a party for her students who have struggled with writing the whole term. Using journals, she has helped them discover their inner voices and is using the celebration as a chance for students to read their writing. One student, who has been in the background, reads an amazing entry and shows his depth of learning.

Learner with special needs: *Mask* (Bogdanovich & Hamilton Phelan, 1985)

Mother talking to principal—The mother tells the principal, in a highly charged scene, about the gifts and talents of her disfigured son and rallies for his rights to a full and robust program to help him reach his potential. The scene shows the boy succeeding in a fairly hostile environment.

Action Option 2: Children's Book Characters

As this chapter illustrated, characters can serve as illuminating metaphors for learner types. While middle and high school teams may shy away from this activity because of the picture-book connotation, PLC teams who take the risk with this activity report surprisingly positive results. To use this activity and other PLC Action Options in the team sessions, the facilitator—a position that often rotates—usually organizes the meeting agenda to focus the time together, but may tap members to orchestrate an activity to highlight the topic under focus. At the beginning of the meeting, the facilitator would read the picture book aloud to the team. Once the group focuses on the metaphorical character, the rest of the discussion flows easily. For initial conversations about sharing differentiation strategies for certain types of learners, using archetypes—rather than specific students—takes the discussion to a more neutral place. These discussions focus on how to best differentiate instruction for various kinds of concerns and specific needs. Following is a summary of several useful resources for the convenience of team members, in addition to those already listed in the chapter.

Advanced learners: *The Dot* (Reynolds, 2006)—Vashti is a frustrated grade school artist who says, "I just CAN'T draw!" When she is encouraged by her teacher to have confidence in her talents, however, the tables turn and Vashti uses the same strategies to inspire a classmate.

Developing or struggling learners: *Thank You, Mr. Falker* (Polacco, 1998)—A young girl struggles through the early grades as she tries to learn how to read. She experiences the frustration and shame that are often part of that disability. Her fifth-grade teacher, Mr. Falker, helps her find the key.

English learners (cultural): *The Rainbow Tulip* (Mora, 1999)—A first-grade Mexican American girl goes by Estelita at home and Stella at school. She's embarrassed by her quiet mother who doesn't speak English and who perseveres in her Mexican customs at home. At the May Day festival, however, Stella discovers how much more colorful her tulip costume is than the single-shade tulip outfits the other girls in her class have made.

English learners (new immigrants): *La Mariposa* (Jímenez, 1998)—The story opens with young Francisco's first day at a new school. His enthusiasm is short lived because he quickly realizes he can't understand a word anyone is saying. The struggle to comprehend a foreign language makes Francisco's head ache. To make matters worse, he inadvertently angers the class bully by accepting the principal's offer of a jacket from the lost and found.

Learners with special needs (physically challenged): *The Acorn People* (Jones, 1996)— This novella is based on the experiences of the author, Ron Jones, who spent a summer shortly after his college graduation as a counselor at a camp for physically challenged kids, Camp Wiggins.

Action Option 3: On a Scale of One to Ten

To process the content in chapter 7, PLC teams can use this scaling strategy. The idea is to self-reflect using a scale of one to ten, with ten as the highest possible rating. Here is a sample question:

> On a scale of one to ten, how would you rate your ability as a classroom teacher to differentiate for the gifted learner?

After the question has been asked and responded to by the team, a facilitator tallies the results on the board and moderates a discussion. For example, the facilitator might ask, "What might you do to raise your rating? Give one example."

The ensuing discussions are focused and engaging because of the data; the scale strategy forces teachers to give their opinions and ideas a numerical score. This simple modification changes a typical staff meeting into a meaningful conversation about instruction. It also demonstrates the power of data-driven conversations.

For example, if teachers agree that, on a scale of one to ten, their average skill of differentiated instruction for the gifted learner is a six, they have valuable information to act on. This helps the next part of that question—How would you raise that score?—become a focused discussion as well.

As with the other PLC Action Options, this activity is appropriate for classroom discussions, too. Following are various examples in several subject areas:

- On a scale of one to ten, how would you rate your behavior in the lunchroom? Explain.

- On a scale of one to ten, how would you rate the decision of the main character in the story? Justify.

- On a scale of one to ten, how would you rate the process taken to solve the math problem? Elaborate.

- On a scale of one to ten, how would you rate your student portfolio? Why?

It is easy to see the many applications teachers might use.

CHAPTER 8

CHANGING LESSONS FOR STUDENT SUCCESS

> **PLC TAKE AWAY**
>
> Learning How Teachers Move Differentiated Lessons From Theory to Practice

When teams working within professional learning communities have the basic theoretical understandings in place, they are ready for the nitty-gritty practice of differentiating their lessons with more insight and intentionality. This chapter presents simple, concrete ways for teachers to differentiate their daily or weekly lessons by applying and implementing the theory of differentiation to classroom instructional practices. It also takes basic lessons and differentiates them with a systematic set of procedures, which show teachers how to turn the theory into an easy-to-use analytical tool. Step-by-step examples make the scaffolding of the process easy to follow. A lesson-plan template is included as well, which PLC teams might find useful to keep initial planning discussions consistent.

The discussions that ensue in the PLC team setting also illustrate how effective the process becomes as teachers share how they incorporate these tools as part of their lesson-planning techniques. Action Options are included at the end of the chapter to jumpstart the work of differentiation.

Lesson Template Design

Up to this point in the text, we have thoroughly discussed the theory of differentiation and unpacked the processes of changing the content, the process, and the product. Now we will illustrate how PLC team members apply these strategies to their everyday lessons. The sample lesson template is a simple and straightforward design that varies slightly from the Hunter lesson design discussed in chapter 5. (Note: Teachers, PLCs, schools, or even districts may have a preferred lesson design template. Whether your team uses this template or its own, it is always helpful to use a similar lesson design when the PLC team members are sharing and comparing lesson ideas.)

The top of the template collects the logistical information about the grade level, subject area, lesson topic, target learning standard, and lesson objective. These last two categories make the objective clear and explicit for teachers and, in turn, for kids. Finally, there is a place to include big ideas and essential questions.

The template includes several fundamental lesson elements including a motivational hook to invite the learners into the learning; a teacher input section for the skills, concepts, and instructions; and a student output section that delineates what the learning interactions should be. In addition, the lesson template has a designated section for the evidence of learning, assessments, and reflections. (See page 146 for a reproducible of this template. Visit **go.solution-tree.com/instruction** to download all reproducibles in this book.)

Teachers design the lesson for the 80 percent of students who learn the information during the original instruction. They include an anticipatory set or hook that gets the students on board—usually something unexpected, exciting, and high energy such as an interesting object, a riddle, or even an invited guest. Then, teachers specify the input of information and instructions. They delineate student interactions and define the product. Finally, they determine the assessment and reflection. This outline describes the basic lesson teachers do over and over again.

To add the differentiation element, teachers go back to that basic lesson and look at the content changes they can make, the varied processes of learning they can use, and the multiple products they can offer as options to ensure student success. Sometimes teachers include another element to the differentiation planning tools—as mentioned in chapter 4, they can color code their lesson plans to designate the parts of the lesson they are differentiating. For example, they might use a red dot to show that they have changes for content, blue for process options, and green for choices in products. It's just a way for them to be more explicit about differentiating in their planning. It's also a way to verify the differentiation they are doing. Coding is an effective tool that helps emphasize the changes. Thus, in the following discussion, the differentiated sections are noted in bold type (starting on page 137) to highlight the parts of the lesson that have been changed. In addition, there is another take on the differentiation coding process in the Action Options at the end of the chapter (page 144).

Grade:	Subject:	Topic:	Standard(s):	Objective(s):
Big Idea(s):		**Essential Question(s):**		
Hook or Anticipatory Set	Motivation			
Teacher Input	Concepts/Skills/Instruction			
Student Output	Learning Interactions			
Evidence of Learning	Product or Performance			
Assessment	Traditional/Portfolio/Performance			
Student Reflection	Metacognitive Moment			

Figure 8.1: Sample lesson template.

Basic Lesson

The sample in this section targets a sixth-grade basic lesson on building vocabulary to illustrate the entire differentiation process (see fig. 8.2, page 136). However, before continuing the discussion, a word of explanation seems warranted for middle and high school PLC teams who may feel that the lesson is too primary to be useful to them. While this sample lesson targets upper elementary students, it serves as a clear and complete model of how teachers can take a basic lesson and differentiate or tweak that lesson to open doors to the many ways students learn. Using this illustration of differentiation, teachers in PLC teams at all levels can clearly see the process used to change the lesson for different learners.

Grade: 6	Subject: Reading	Topic: Vocabulary	Standard(s): Genre	Objective(s): Vocabulary
Big Idea(s): Reading builds vocabulary		**Essential Question(s):** How does reading various genres build vocabulary?		
Hook or Anticipatory Set	Read one children's book about school: *Testing Miss Malarkey.*			
Teacher Input	One way to learn vocabulary is through extensive reading.			
Student Output	Play Vocabulary Search by finding seven significant words to define and illustrate on cards.			
Evidence of Learning	Write a paragraph using all the new vocabulary words.			
Assessment	Read the book to a primary student using vocabulary flash cards.			
Student Reflection	Fill out a comment card with the pluses and minuses of reading to build vocabulary.			

Figure 8.2: Sample basic lesson.

With that said, the learning standard focuses on the ability of students to be exposed to and to be able read a specific genre (children's literature) with fluency and comprehension. The learning objective is to learn new words—build vocabulary—through different kinds of reading within the genre. The big ideas students take away include that reading builds vocabulary, and reading widely generates a rich vocabulary. Finally, the essential question asks how reading helps students learn vocabulary.

The lesson begins with the teacher introducing an illustrated book about school, *Testing Miss Malarkey* (Finchler, 2000), to hook the sixth graders' natural curiosity, since they don't normally have access to the genre of picture books in reading class. The book usually causes a stir of excitement, as well as an air of importance, once the students understand they will be reading to younger children. These books are very different than the anthology of reading selections and library books they usually read. The teacher then talks about how reading is a great way to build vocabulary and asks students to read the book sometime during the week. The teacher explains that the students are to play a game, Vocabulary Search, after reading the book. They are to select seven new words to place on vocabulary cards. They are then to write a paragraph using their chosen words. As a final part of the lesson, the students read the book to a younger student or classroom, using the vocabulary cards as flash cards before and after the reading. Finally, students share the pluses and minuses of the lesson on a card to be turned in to the teacher.

For the sake of the clarity, the differentiation process for this sample lesson begins with changing the content, then moves to changing the process, and finally to changing the product. Each differentiated element is explained in text and is bolded in the figure.

Changing the Content

To change the content in the basic lesson, teachers usually look at two elements: the hook and the input. In this case, the change to content is made by changing the resources in the hook (see fig. 8.3). Instead of one children's book about school, students are offered a variety of books. For instance, *Testing Miss Malarkey*; *Thank You, Mr. Falker*; *The Fine, Fine School*; *The First Days of School*; *Through the Cracks*; and *Miss Nelson Is Missing!* Teachers cite choice and challenge as reasons for giving resource options. Nothing else is changed, but notice how this one change really opens up the lesson for different learners. They now have a set of books to choose from as they weigh their options for the assignment.

Grade: 6	Subject: Reading	Topic: Vocabulary	Standard(s): Genre	Objective(s): Vocabulary
Big Idea(s): Reading builds vocabulary		**Essential Question(s):** How does reading various genres build vocabulary?		
Hook or Anticipatory Set	Read one children's book about school: *Testing Miss Malarkey*; *Thank you, Mr. Falker*; *The Fine, Fine School*; *The First Days of School*; *Through the Cracks*; or *Miss Nelson is Missing!* **Change the content by changing the resources.**			
Teacher Input	One way to learn vocabulary is through extensive reading.			
Student Output	Play Vocabulary Search by finding seven significant words to define and illustrate on cards.			
Evidence of Learning	Write a paragraph using all the new vocabulary words.			
Assessment	Read the book to a primary student using vocabulary flash cards.			
Student Reflection	Fill out a comment card with the pluses and minuses of reading to build vocabulary.			

Figure 8.3: Sample basic lesson with content change.

By making simple changes in the content—in this case, by changing the resources with a variety of books—students can choose the book that appeals to their interests and levels. Offering different resources is truly one of the easiest and most effective ways to differentiate instruction. Next, we'll look at differentiating processes.

Changing the Process

When teachers look at ways to change the process, they consider changing elements of direct instruction, adding structures for cooperative learning, or using inquiry for investigations and explorations. In this lesson, teachers now focus on the student interactions and student reflections. As depicted in figure 8.4, they have chosen to differentiate the process through interaction—the student assignment now includes working cooperatively with a partner. Instead of just identifying seven new words, students must agree on the book and words they select. In addition, the partners reflect and dialogue about the pluses and minuses of the strategy of reading to build vocabulary.

Grade: 6	Subject: Reading	Topic: Vocabulary	Standard(s): Genre	Objective(s): Vocabulary
Big Idea(s): Reading builds vocabulary	**Essential Question(s):** How does reading various genres build vocabulary?			
Hook or Anticipatory Set	Read one children's book about school: *Testing Miss Malarkey*; *Thank you, Mr. Falker*; *The Fine, Fine School*; *The First Days of School*; *Through the Cracks*; or *Miss Nelson is Missing!* **Change the content by changing the resources.**			
Teacher Input	One way to learn vocabulary is through extensive reading.			
Student Output	Play Vocabulary Search by reading a book with a partner and deciding, together, on seven words; as a pair, create word cards to define and illustrate the words. **Change the process by requiring cooperative pairs.**			
Evidence of Learning	Write a paragraph using all the new vocabulary words.			
Assessment	Read the book to a primary student using vocabulary flash cards.			
Student Reflection	Comment on the pluses and minuses of reading to build vocabulary and on working together. **Change the process by working as partners and reflecting on teamwork.**			

Figure 8.4: Sample basic lesson with content and process changes.

Again, by differentiating the process to include cooperative partners, the lesson offers increased learning opportunities for students who have strong interpersonal skills as well as for students who may need the support of a partner to succeed at the tasks. These simple differentiation techniques, this tweaking of a basic lesson by changing the process, are the essence of what teachers do to ensure student success.

Changing the Product

In a third modification, teachers in the PLC teams change the product by changing the entry point, exit point, or by changing the accountability option (see fig. 8.5, page 140). In the template, teachers focus on the lesson elements of product and assessment. In the example lesson for sixth graders, the changes in product involve three choices in addition to the original choice of writing a paragraph. Students can choose any one of the following as their product or evidence of learning: a paragraph (verbal), a booklet of images made from folded paper (bodily), a concept map or graphic organizer of the words (visual), or a word puzzle (mathematical). In addition, teachers offer an assessment that requires self-reflection and self-assessment using a checklist of three criteria: (1) preparation, (2) presentation, and (3) new vocabulary.

By changing the product with multimodal options, and by changing the assessment with a criteria checklist or a short paragraph, different students can go to their modality of strength and use a self-assessment tool that scaffolds the learning by identifying three criteria to consider.

Teachers enhance the lessons and make them more accessible to the talents and needs of learners by adding these kinds of differentiation techniques. These efforts toward differentiated lessons become intentional and purposeful as the teachers in PLCs become more reflective. They know what they want students to learn, they try to ensure that all students have a way to learn it, and they identify explicit changes to the content, process, and product through techniques such as color-coding technique (or bold type in this case).

Another kind of coding focuses on learner archetypes. For developing or struggling learners, an arrow pointing down signifies differentiation to simplify the learning, while an arrow pointing up signifies differentiation to challenge advanced learners. In turn, a horizontal arrow signifies differentiation to enhance learning for English learners. Although some teachers object to the arrow codes because they might reveal motives or be interpreted as a lesson being "dummied down," coding is quite helpful early in the differentiation process. It is simply an option to consider.

Grade: 6	Subject: Reading	Topic: Vocabulary	Standard(s): Genre	Objective(s): Vocabulary
Big Idea(s): Reading builds vocabulary		**Essential Question(s):** How does reading various genres build vocabulary?		
Hook or Anticipatory Set	Read one children's book about school: *Testing Miss Malarkey; Thank you, Mr. Falker; The Fine, Fine School; The First Days of School; Through the Cracks;* or *Miss Nelson is Missing!* **Change the content by changing the resources.**			
Teacher Input	One way to learn vocabulary is through extensive reading.			
Student Output	Play Vocabulary Search by reading a book with a partner and deciding, together, on seven words; as a pair, create word cards to define and illustrate the words. **Change the process by requiring cooperative pairs.**			
Evidence of Learning	Each partner uses all the words in one of the following: • A paragraph (verbal) • A story in a booklet made from folded paper (bodily) • A map or graphic organizer of the words (visual) • A word puzzle (mathematical) **Change the product with multimodal options.**			
Assessment	Share by reading the book to a primary classroom and use flash cards with the younger students; mark the checklist on your performance, or write a short paragraph about the pluses and minuses (and any questions you might have) regarding preparation, presentation, and new vocabulary. **Change the product by changing the accountability method.**			
Student Reflection	Comment on the pluses and minuses of reading to build vocabulary and on working together. **Change the process by working as partners and reflecting on teamwork.**			

Figure 8.5: Sample basic lesson with content, process, and product changes.

As a final scaffolding piece, we've included various templates for PLCs to review and enhance as they practice using the principles and tools of differentiation. Principles include change, challenge, and choice. Tools help change the content, process, and products to meet student readiness levels, personal interests, and learning profiles. Following are three sample lesson starters, one each for elementary (fig. 8.6), middle (fig. 8.7, page 142), and high school (fig. 8.8, page 143).

Elementary Lesson

The elementary-level basic lesson is a fifth-grade social studies lesson based on the highly informative book *How a Bill Becomes a Law* (Van Wie, 1999). The basic lesson plan is a bare-bones traditional approach. The bolded text suggests differentiated elements that open the lesson options to a variety of strengths and weaknesses. In addition, there are many activities within *How a Bill Becomes a Law* to explore.

Grade: 5	Subject: Social studies	Topic: Legislature	Standard(s): Government	Objective(s): Bill to law
Big Idea(s): Government by the people		Essential Question(s): How do citizens enact laws?		
Hook or Anticipatory Set	Present list of silly, obsolete laws still on the books as a "Did you know . . ." game (see Collier, 2008, for ideas), such as the following: • Connecticut—In Devon, it is illegal to walk backward after sunset. • Kentucky—Throwing tomatoes at a public speaker is punishable by up to one year in jail. • Georgia—It is illegal to carry an ice cream cone in one's back pocket if it is Sunday. • Illinois—In Chicago, it is illegal to eat in any building that is currently on fire.			
Teacher Input	Review two houses of Congress; teach the seven steps from a bill to a law: 1. Congress introduces bill. 2. Committee considers the bill. 3. Subcommittee holds hearing. 4. Both houses debate and refer bill. 5. Committee conferences to compromise bill. 6. Members vote yes or no. 7. If two-thirds vote yes, the president either signs the bill into law or vetoes it. **Change the content by showing a film of the process (resources).**			
Student Output	Create a booklet telling the story of a bill becoming law. **Change the process through research by following a bill to law (inquiry).**			
Evidence of Learning	Share booklet with a peer partner and turn it in. **Change the product by creating a storyboard, slide show, scripted role-play, or song (multimodal).**			
Assessment	Grade booklet and send home for student to share with family. **Change the product by developing checklists and rubrics (accountability).**			
Student Reflection	Discuss what was hard and what was easy about the assignment.			

Figure 8.6: Elementary lesson on how a bill becomes a law.

Middle School Lesson

The example for a middle school lesson focuses on building skills in estimation and mental math. Looking at the lesson design in figure 8.7, note the bold type designating the differentiated instructional options that provide various entry points and expressive modes for a diverse seventh-grade classroom.

Grade: 7	Subject: Math	Topic: Estimation/ mental math	Standard(s): Computational skills	Objective(s): Computation accuracy
Big Idea(s): Numbers count		Essential Question(s): How are estimation and mental math useful?		
Hook or Anticipatory Set	Start with a series of mental math problems for the whole class.			
Teacher Input	Discuss strategies for estimating or guesstimating in your head: rounding off, comparing, chunking, thinking with the end in mind, and so on. **Change the content by inviting a guest business speaker from the community (resources).**			
Student Output	Have students solve mental problems in a timed interaction. **Change the process by working in pairs (cooperative structures).**			
Evidence of Learning	Create real-world problem scenarios where mental math and estimating skills are needed: shopping, painting a room, travel distances and times, and so on. **Change the product by creating a game board, a brain science report, or a Jeopardy game relating to estimation and mental math (multimodal).**			
Assessment	Provide an end-of-chapter test covering estimation and mental math problem solving. **Change the product by offering an oral quiz option for the final assessment (accountability).**			
Student Reflection	Students write a one- to three-sentence reflection on the activity. **Change the product by completing the journal stem or complete the following mediated journal entry (accountability).** **1. Name someone who is good at math (personal acquaintance, historical figure, fictional character).** **2. Describe two traits of the person.** **3. Describe someone who is not very good at math.** **4. Tell how the two people are different.** **5. Write a concluding sentence.** **6. Give your piece a telling title.**			

Figure 8.7: Middle school lesson on estimation and mental math.

High School Lesson

The high school example focuses on a literature lesson about paradox and ambiguity. Again, this example is a mere lesson outline; the opportunities for differentiating instruction are noted in bolded text.

Grade: 10	Subject: English literature	Topic: Swift's *A Modest Proposal*	Standard(s): Literature	Objective(s): Literary elements
Big Idea(s): Things are not always what they seem		**Essential Question(s):** How do literary elements enhance or detract from the reading?		
Hook or Anticipatory Set	Show M. C. Escher's optical illusions to demonstrate ambiguity in a visually obvious way. **Change the content by showing various examples of ambiguity, paradox, and irony through optical illusions, political cartoons, riddles, and jokes (resources).**			
Teacher Input	Present definitions and examples of ambiguity, paradox, and irony in literature. **Change the content in three ways (complexity). Concrete: Remove a vest from under a jacket without removing the jacket. Symbolic: View optical illusions and describe the phenomena. Abstract: Read selections of ambiguous passages, paradoxical events, and dramatic irony.**			
Student Output	Find examples of ambiguity, paradox, and irony in Swift's *A Modest Proposal*. **Change the process by using a jigsaw activity (cooperative learning). Divide class into groups of three and have each member research one of the literary elements—ambiguity, paradox, and irony—and share information in the threesome with an interactive strategy using three modalities.**			
Evidence of Learning	Write an expository essay about ambiguity, paradox, or irony. **Change the product by using a bingo board and working in pairs to decide on the evidence of learning. Have the pairs select three of the nine options in a bingo row—slide show, board game, readings, film clip, research report, role-play, optical illusion drawing, or original idea. Once the pairs have three selections, they decide together which one they will do (modality).**			
Assessment	Read a selected piece of literature; identify ambiguity, paradox, or irony; and explain fully. Critique whether or not it worked for the reader. **Change the product by selecting from the final selections from the bingo choice board and critiquing the effectiveness of its use (accountability).**			
Student Reflection	Dialogue with two peers—each member reflects on one of the literary elements.			

Figure 8.8: High school lesson on literature.

This brief delineation of the differentiation process demonstrates how easy it is to revisit a basic lesson and change the content, process, and product. It should also be evident that differentiating the lesson truly does enhance the lesson. Each time a teacher reviews the lesson, especially as part of a PLC team, he or she discovers ways to add depth and breadth to the learning. The team's reservoir of activities creates many options for different kinds of learners. In fact, teachers who are part of PLCs are usually energized by this kind of planning. They sense the power of these reflective conversations to improve and enhance their own teaching.

Action Options

> **PLC TAKE AWAY**
>
> Learning How Teachers Move Differentiated Lessons From Theory to Practice

A good beginning step, mentioned throughout this book, is for PLC members to first look over lessons that they currently teach and to label or code their differentiation strategies. This affirmation helps encourage further differentiation. When teachers can recognize how they already make planning decisions, based on the different types of students they teach, they feel empowered and will want to explore new ways to reach and teach all of their students.

As a PLC matures and its teams become focused on the essential questions—what they want students to know, how they will know when students know it, and what they will do when student don't know it—pragmatic concerns surface. Teachers start looking for ways to ensure that what they are teaching is accessible to all the students in their care. They embrace differentiation as a powerful instructional tool, they are motivated to use formative assessments and to create common assessments, and they collaborate willingly to impact their daily planning and teaching. These are the signs that teams are moving into highly functioning teams within evolving professional learning communities.

Included in this discussion on lesson design for differentiated instruction are two Action Options to consider. That's a Good Idea is an affirming activity, and Pass the Lesson uses the lesson design template to revisit, review, and use! Visit www .allthingsplc.info/wordpress/?p=50 for information on working within a PLC to create a robust curriculum unit.

Action Option 1: That's a Good Idea

This strategy adds structure to discussions about individual lesson designs and promotes a positive attitude for members of PLCs.

Teachers take turns explaining a basic lesson and then give one specific example of how the lesson is differentiated. For instance, they might show how—and explain why—they changed the process. As members share their lessons and the rationale for their decisions, other members can only answer by using the sentence stem *That's a good idea because . . .* completed with specific examples. Before someone can respond, he or she has to have listened actively and understood well enough to comment constructively. For example, if a teacher is explaining how he changed the learning process by having students research in the library in cooperative pairs, instead of someone saying, "Why didn't you also change the resources by letting the students research online?," she would say, "That's a good idea because when students work in pairs, they can support each other in the resource search." It is simultaneously an affirming activity and a sharing activity.

Action Option 2: Pass the Lesson

Previously in this chapter, an example of a sixth-grade lesson template showed how, in a step-by-step process, a teacher could differentiate the content, process, and product. Now we will show how teachers from similar subjects or grades can pair and create a basic lesson using that template.

To begin, it is best if the lesson is written out using poster paper and if all of the writing for the initial lesson is done in one color of ink, for clarity.

Next, each pair passes its basic lesson to another pair. This pair of teachers looks over their new lesson and, using a different color marker, differentiates the content. This step should take three to four minutes. This process of passing continues until all of the lessons have been differentiated for content, process, and product. Depending on how many people are participating, some pairs of teachers will not get their own lessons passed back until all three parts are differentiated by their colleagues.

Pass the Lesson helps teachers focus on how to differentiate rather than on content or grade level. Looking at lesson plans created by colleagues and seeing the choices they made to differentiate for content, process, and product is illuminating for teachers. This strategy takes the concepts of differentiation and anchors them in concrete examples developed by teachers working toward a common goal.

Lesson Template

Grade:	Subject:	Topic:	Standard(s):	Objective(s):

Big Idea(s):	Essential Question(s):

Hook or Anticipatory Set	Motivation
Teacher Input	Concepts/Skills/Instruction
Student Output	Learning Interactions
Evidence of Learning	Product or Performance
Assessment	Traditional/Portfolio/Performance
Student Reflection	Metacognitive Moment

CHAPTER 9

CHANGING UNITS FOR STUDENT SUCCESS

PLC TAKE AWAY

Learning How Teachers Move Differentiated Curriculum Units From Theory to Practice

As with collaborative lesson planning, another effective target task for teachers within professional learning communities is collaborative development of curriculum *units* with built-in differentiation. As teachers work together in PLCs, they share ways to use a multimodal planning grid for units of study that have many diverse options for student assignments. Designing the curriculum unit uses the basic principles of differentiation—change, challenge, and choice—as a guide, just as lesson planning does. To explore this topic, we've included sample curriculum units for elementary, middle, and high school levels. At the end of the chapter, Action Options are listed to help lead the learning community teams through this instructional initiative.

To begin the process of curriculum planning, we introduce a multimodal unit planning template, referred to as a multimodal curriculum grid of activities. This template is a useful tool for PLC teams as they collaborate and generate ideas for rich, robust, and rigorous curriculum units. In fact, the grid basically drives the conversation to multimodal thinking. This planning is done in the content areas such as English, social studies, science, math, and sometimes as a cross-disciplinary unit of study designed around conceptual themes (change, conflict, invention, and so on).

Whatever the context of the units, the focus is on developing a grand scheme that provides as many differentiated instructional opportunities as possible.

Multimodal Curriculum Grid of Activities

The multimodal curriculum grid of activities captures the initial decisions that teachers make when planning a curriculum unit. Typical elements for the curriculum grid include general unit information (grade level, subjects, topics, standards, big-idea themes, essential questions) and the actual grid itself, which delineates various activity options and assessments.

Incorporating Unit Information

Teachers within PLC teams, which may consist of grade-level or department colleagues, begin developing the curriculum unit grid of differentiated activities by defining the information required. The first step is to state the grade-level focus, subject, and target topic. They should use large poster paper so all members of the team can see the work as it unfolds. It is important to note that the team is not creating a new curriculum; instead, the teachers are simply developing a more differentiated approach to existing curricular requirements based on the standards of learning of their grade levels or disciplines.

Next, the team considers the specific student learning standards targeted in this curriculum unit. The PLC teams discuss this element in detail, as this is what they want students to learn. As they look at the essential or power standards of the curriculum, they consider content and process standards as well. *Content standards* are the many standards that unpack the subject matter within the discipline, while the *process standards* are often the life skills of problem solving, research, and communication. It is critical that the standards of the unit are agreed upon by the team and are clearly delineated in the curriculum document.

Once the topic is in focus and the standards of learning are discussed and agreed upon, the PLC teams are ready to identify the *big ideas* that permeate the unit. Again, the collective wisdom of the team propels this conversation, as relevant ideas are put on the table. In the process of uncovering the themes that thread through the unit, teachers often move far beyond the facts, data, and information and into more global or universal ideas that provide enduring learnings (Wiggins & McTighe, 2005).

In a similar vein, as the PLCs address *essential questions* that drive the curriculum unit, they naturally unpack the content, but they also tend to unpack the essence of the unit that moves beyond the specific subject matter and into the realm of life learning. For example, a unit on World War II may have essential questions about specific outcomes of events and particular leadership motives, yet the essential questions may also inquire about the paradox of waging war for the goal of peace.

It is often in these lively discussions about big ideas and essential questions that the unit starts to come alive and the PLC teams get excited about teaching the unit. They also get involved with the process of their own professional learning and are energized by the collaborative spirit of the work.

One final note on the template details: it is recommended that the big ideas be made more student friendly by adding a *tagline* to the theme. The tagline is a catchy phrase that restates the more formal topic or concept of the unit; it takes the curriculum term and adds a more inviting phrase. For example, "Democracy—Who Rules?" takes the formal word, *democracy*, and unpacks it with the question "Who Rules?" Taglines often emerge spontaneously, as part of discussions on essential questions. In "Government—We the People," *government* is the unit focus, while "We the People" is the tagline that illuminates the focus in student-friendly terminology. For instance, taglines might look like the following:

- Plants—It's Not Easy Being Green
- Cycles—What Goes 'Round, Comes 'Round
- Weather—In the Eye of the Storm
- Phonics—Sounds Good to Me
- Genetics—"I Yam Who I Yam"
- Exploration—Did You Know?

Sometimes the tagline becomes a refrain that weaves throughout the unit of study. It may even echo a song that threads through the entire unit. In sum, taglines work for any age group, because they provide insight into the curriculum topic. They should be generated by the teachers or the students so they are age-appropriate and add a little spice and sense of ownership to the subject matter.

Developing Activity Options

Once teams have discussed these fundamental issues, they turn their attention to the development of the activity options grid. This grid of activities uses Gardner's (1999) eight multiple intelligences or learning preferences, because they are a natural organizer for generating multimodal ideas. The grid becomes a giant choice board of sorts. As such, it has options that appeal to different types of learners with varied strengths and weaknesses in their learning profiles.

With the grid of options completed, teachers and students have a rich bank of ideas to consider as they plot a path of learning. Teachers can design assignments for all students and simultaneously target specific assignments for certain students. Teachers can also conference with the kids individually and let students choose from a number of activity options, as long as there is guidance and explanations of expectations for accountability. In developing curriculum units with explicit attention to multimodal options, teachers in PLCs are anticipating the talents and needs of their students as much as they are anticipating the content they will teach. They are practicing student-centered, student-driven schooling that ensures the success of the students in their care.

In developing multimodal curriculum units, the adage "A picture is worth a thousand words" holds true. The following grid of options (fig. 9.1, page 152) is an initial curriculum framework that teachers revisit many times as they develop the various activity options named in the cells. Please note that the grid is laid out with the multiple intelligences or learning style preferences in a specific sequence. We reference this arrangement as *VIM N B*, a take on vim 'n' vigor. It serves as a quick memory cue to the eight modalities exemplified by Gardner's multiple intelligences: verbal/linguistic, visual/spatial, interpersonal/social, intrapersonal/self, mathematical/logical, musical/rhythmic, naturalist/physical world, and bodily/kinesthetic.

The curriculum unit used in figure 9.1 is just a planner, a placeholder for ideas, as noted earlier. As the teachers work with the grid, they will revisit it many times as they elaborate on actual lessons that will eventually be developed and differentiated. Also, please note that the grid can be done with the PLC teams on large poster paper, using sticky notes for the various ideas. In this way, there is no limit to the number of ideas that teachers generate in the initial team brainstorm. Of course, individual teachers can use the grid on a regular piece of paper to start the process on their own.

This eighth-grade social studies example focuses on democracy and addresses social studies standards on developing democratic values. One big idea that surfaces is the theme of "life, liberty, and the pursuit of happiness" from the U.S. Declaration of Independence. A student-friendly tagline could be "Democracy—United We Stand." The essential question guiding the unit development is, "How do democratic values guide civic actions?"

It's obvious, even at this beginning point, that good conversation and collaboration go into such rich results. The opportunities for activity options are already emerging with the mention of primary documents—the U.S. Declaration of Independence and Constitution. As the brainstorm of activities ensues, teachers tap into their expertise and experiences and start inundating the conversation with proven activities and learning options. From verbal activities involving written essays and reading rounds, to musical activities studying composers of national songs, to creating raps about historical information, and onto carouseling activities in which students move from station to station, the grid unfolds in all its glory. It is a learning experience for all involved.

Identifying Assessment Options

As in all good curricular planning, instructional activities should also be intertwined with the assessment options in the process of curriculum unit development. As the teachers in PLC teams talk about assessment options, they should deliberately include activities that require traditional quizzes and criterion-referenced testing, activities that lend themselves to real or virtual portfolios, and robust products and performances that require a scoring rubric of criteria and indicators of quality. By offering differentiated instructional activity and assessment options, teachers purposefully provide learning and accountability choices for developing and advanced learners, for English learners, and for learners with special needs.

PLC teams can now use the synergy of the "team think" to identify or generate assessment options that offer balance among the three assessment categories: traditional assessments, portfolio assessments, and performance assessments. At this stage, the teachers look over the grid and flag certain items that can be used as evidence of learning. Using a coding process, they tag items in the grid as potential assessment options. For example, they mark cells that might develop into a traditional assessment with a *T*, items that can be integrated into a student portfolio (or "folio") with an *F*, and cells that call for a performance assessment with a *P*:

- Traditional assessments—grades and ranking via tests, quizzes, and work samples

- Folio assessments—growth and development via drafts, biography of a work, products

- Performance assessments—transfer and application via performance tasks and scoring rubrics

Again, this is a preliminary team planner, and many details need to be worked out as the unit planning proceeds.

For a quick example to illustrate the process, we've coded certain activities in figure 9.1 (page 152) based on assessment options: concept map of government, small-group investigations, and timelines of democratic victories have been marked with a *T*; storyboard of historical democratic events, biographical portfolio of a project, and U.S. map have been marked with an *F*; and study of primary documents, panel debate, rap writing, and role-play of democracy at work have been marked with a *P*. The assessment appraisal is an initial way to ensure that assessment options are built into each unit of study, although they still may need full development at another time. Again, this is a team planning tool that expedites the work of PLCs when they do have time together. It is only a first stab at the curriculum development; each idea is eventually unpacked with the lesson design elements. (See page 159 for a reproducible of the grid template, and pages 160–161 for help in brainstorming for each intelligence. Visit **go.solution-tree.com/instruction** to download all reproducibles in this book.)

Grade: 8	Subject: Social studies		Topic(s): Democracy		Standard(s): Democratic values		
Big Ideas: Life, liberty, and the pursuit of happiness							
Tagline: Democracy—United We Stand					Essential Question: How do democratic values guide civic actions?		
Verbal	**Visual**	**Interpersonal**	**Intrapersonal**	**Mathematical**	**Musical**	**Naturalist**	**Bodily**
Participate in a reader's theater.	Create a concept map of government **(T)**.	Set up a panel debate **(P)**.	Keep journals.	Look at demographics.	Write a rap **(P)**.	Classify roles and responsibilities of citizens.	Draw a U.S. map **(F)**.
Write an essay on three branches of government.	Watch a film on presidents.	Participate in a reader's theater.	Keep learning logs.	Survey democratic values.	Listen to marches and compare and contrast them.	List civic duties in community, school, and home.	Identify red states and blue states.
Play a vocabulary game.	Make a photo gallery of notable historical figures.	Jigsaw a chapter in a social studies text.	Create a biographical portfolio of a project **(F)**.	Learn statistics about current issues in Congress.	Learn national songs of various countries.	Study environmental issues.	Model a democratic government.
Read a biography.	Create posters and billboards.	Participate in small-group investigations **(T)**.	Write personal reflections.	Make statistical projections and guesses.	Learn the national anthem of your country.	Study the political landscape.	Visit the capitol.
Find and study primary documents **(P)**.	Analyze political cartoons.	Use the carouseling activity for puppets and speeches.	Introduce and promote Habits of Mind.	Compare democracy to dictatorship.	Study composers.	Get involved in the community.	Create a foldable book of historic documents.
Read narrative stories.	Create a storyboard of historical democratic events **(F)**.	Participate in human graphs on democracy issues in the news.	Read case studies for values clarification.	Draw timelines of democratic victories **(T)**.	Write limericks as promotional video ads for democracy.	Learn state flowers and birds.	Role-play or act out a dramatic scene of democracy at work **(P)**.
Listen to books on CD.	Find interesting, topical websites.	Participate in an agree-disagree think-pair-share.	Access character education principles.	Make a flow chart of a bill becoming law.	Stage a class musical.	Visit a court of law.	Develop a puppet show on personal rights.

Figure 9.1: Sample multimodal curriculum unit planning template.

The curriculum grid development can easily be done in three forty-five-minute sessions with PLCs. The first session focuses on the content, standards, big ideas, and essential questions; the second session is geared toward the brainstorm of activity options; and the third session is devoted to planning for balanced assessment options that are integrated throughout the unit. With this dynamic planning tool for collaboration that forces attention toward multimodal learning activities, the unit evolves with a freshness and excitement that teachers and students can easily rally around. In fact, after PLC teams become familiar with the multimodal planning grid, teachers sometimes ask students to use the topic and big ideas to brainstorm a title and tagline for the curriculum unit. This is a powerful, student-centered involvement strategy that gets huge buy-in from the students.

Multimodal Grid Examples

With the lesson template—or a premade template of their choosing—and the multimodal curriculum grid, PLC teams talk together, share together, plan together, and reflect together. Over time, as the teams develop differentiated lessons and units, they start to accumulate completed artifacts that they can revisit with new information and viable strategies. If archived online for future use, this lesson design and unit planning work will serve future projects as well. In addition, these completed differentiated grids can be shared across the building and across the district for PLC teams beginning their work on differentiated instruction.

Following are three curriculum unit frames to review as part of a PLC practice exercise: elementary school (fig. 9.2, page 155), middle school (fig. 9.3, page 156), and high school (fig. 9.4, page 157). The three distinct levels have been included to show that a completed grid of multimodal activities is possible for all age groups. It is often easier to see the transfer and application if teams have an example at their level and with their typical content. In addition, while these grids have activities listed in every cell, the PLC teams might list more activities as they review the grid and ideas occur to them by association or piggybacking on the information, which is how brainstorming works when teams are actually developing a grid. It is always easier to add to an existing sample than to start from scratch.

PLC teams should code these assessment options by marking a *T* on all cells that might develop into a traditional assessment, an *F* on items in each column for portfolio or "folio" items, and a *P* on cells that call for a performance assessment with a scoring rubric of criteria and quality indicators.

The example for elementary school (page 155) is an earth science unit, in which students study the three categories of rocks. PLC teams brainstorm multimodal activities to provide differentiated options to the curriculum unit. Again, this grid is an initial planning tool that acts as a catalyst. In addition, the session becomes quite motivational for teachers as they see the potential of the unit for the students.

The middle school example (page 156) centers on a high-interest topic for early adolescents—the Olympic Games. While it is a social studies unit, it offers opportunities for math, science, art, music, and sports. It is ripe for multimodal learning that is inherently differentiated.

The high school example (page 157) centers on the topic of African American history. Similar topics may be more appropriate for various countries. It offers opportunities to learn in various content areas including social studies, math, science, art, music, business, health, and physical education. This grid is rich with opportunities for multimodal learning that are differentiated by the very nature of the tasks.

A quick glance at the samples shows how the PLC process of brainstorming a multimodal grid of activity options supports differentiated instruction. The multimodal options are literally woven throughout the grid, creating a rich, robust unit.

Groups of students may be assigned a "path" through the grid, with certain modalities selected intentionally by the teacher. Students may also be given choices of activities. Any combination of teacher-assigned or student-selected activities could become available once the grid is developed. It is a flexible planning tool that lends itself to varied applications. Again, this is a team planning tool that ignites the unit planning process. Much detail is required as the implementation of the unit unfolds.

Action Options

PLC TAKE AWAY

Learning How Teachers Move Differentiated Curriculum Units From Theory to Practice

---

As PLCs evolve, so do the teams of teachers working within the community; but their priorities do not change. Their mission continues to be a commitment to collaborative inquiry and achievement of better results for the children they serve. As the individual teams of educators evolve, however, they can begin to pursue this mission at the level of curriculum design, as well as instructional design. Embedded in these curriculum units are all of the research-based attributes of differentiated instruction. Because these units are designed holistically by classroom teachers—rather than by prescribed, top-down models—they create buy-in. In addition, these larger, more complex curriculum units comprise a collection of practical strategies, tested and improved by the very classroom teachers who will implement them.

Grade: 3	Subject: Earth science		Topic(s): Rocks		Standard(s): Geology		

Big Ideas: Sustainable elements
Tagline: Rock solid

Essential Question: How do we preserve and enhance the earth we have inherited?

Verbal	Visual	Interpersonal	Intrapersonal	Mathematical	Musical	Naturalist	Bodily
Read nonfiction.	Draw rock types.	Visit quarry or local site.	Keep a log of excursion notes.	Graph resources.	Watch *Rock of Ages*.	Sort and classify rock samples.	Create model mudslide.
Read a science text.	Watch topical shows on the History Channel.	Write report on minerals and gems with a partner.	Learn birthstones.	Draw a timeline of rock formations.	Make primitive instruments out of rocks.	Collect rocks in an egg carton.	Create relief maps.
Participate in a reader's theater.	Watch *The Flintstones* cartoon characters.	Jigsaw rock types.	Make pet rock.	Debate on the benefits and detriments of different types of rocks.	Study rock and roll.	Study volcanoes, earthquakes, and waterfalls.	Study gems by classifying them.
Learn topical vocabulary.	Create a storyboard.	Participate in an agree-disagree think-pair-share.	Make a personal mosaic.	Weigh rock samples.	Play on concept of *Rock of Ages* by listening for music appreciation through the ages.	Study pyramids.	Participate in an archeological dig.
Write.	Draw diagrams.	Participate in a tear-share activity.	Draw rock signs depicting differences in personalities, similar to astrology.	Learn about the gold standard.	Stage a performance.	Take a geological field trip.	Sculpt with clay.
Write poetry—a cinquain (five-line poem) or a haiku.	Create charts or illustrations of rock formations.	Participate in an AB partner pyramid game.	Keep a log of rock types, feel, hardness, and shapes.	Use appropriate technology software to learn about rocks, earth science, volcanoes, and so on.	Listen to soothing nature music—water flowing, wind, bird songs.	Visit a natural history museum.	Study rock carvings.
Research on the Internet.	View video of natural occurrences such as earthquakes and volcanoes.	Set up stations to hear sample reports.	Find a rock and write a personal statement on it.	Test and record data.	Create water sounds with a sculpture.	Make an excursion to a quarry.	Study pottery making.

Figure 9.2: Elementary school curriculum unit on earth science.

| Grade: 7 | Subject: Social studies | | Topic(s): Olympic Games | | Standard(s): Interdependence | | |

Big Ideas: Personal best
Tagline: Be the best that you can be
Essential Question: How do you achieve personal goals?

Verbal	Visual	Interpersonal	Intrapersonal	Mathematical	Musical	Naturalist	Bodily
Learn about foreign languages.	Create visual symbols.	Focus on teamwork.	Set goals.	Make maps.	Learn national songs.	Study health and wellness.	Practice yoga.
Read a narrative or biography.	Create posters.	Focus on team building.	Set goals for personal best.	Compute data about sporting events.	Listen to cultural music.	Exercise.	Build models.
Read and write nonfiction about champions.	Paint murals.	Coach peers and be coached by peers.	Keep a diary of training.	Compile athlete country data.	Write an Olympic rap.	Learn and do cardiovascular exercises.	Make illustrations.
Write an Olympic bid proposal.	Watch a topical film.	Train with partners.	Keep a log of exercise, diet, and relaxation.	Compile athlete statistics.	Write Olympic-themed limericks.	Study the climate, temperatures, and altitude of various countries.	Learn about ergonomics.
Write letters.	Create advertisements.	Become pen pals or email buddies.	Create an electronic personal portfolio Web page.	Calculate travel budgets.	Listen to music as a complement to exercise.	Learn about the human body.	Incorporate movement into an activity.
Learn Olympic vocabulary.	Make collages.	Use the Internet to find a global partner for dialogue about goals.	Put together a photo album of sports and interests.	Research champions.	Use background music.	Study countries and regions.	Perform cultural dances.
Invent a persuasive new sport.	Stream videos.	Use video conferences.	Write down strengths and weaknesses.	Access Internet for information about sports figures, games, and results.	Perform with culturally diverse instruments.	Use classifying as a way to sort the various sports and games.	Participate in relays.

Figure 9.3: Middle school curriculum unit on Olympic Games.

Grade: 11	Subject: American studies		Topic(s): African American history		Standard(s): History, cultures		
Big Ideas: Individual rights and freedoms			Essential Question: How is the United States a mosaic and a melting pot?				
Tagline: Stand tall and be heard							
Verbal	Visual	Interpersonal	Intrapersonal	Mathematical	Musical	Naturalist	Bodily
Read the "I have a dream" speech.	Create a display of weapons.	Study the Dred Scott case.	Read the diary of a slave.	Compile local data.	Listen to soul music.	Collect primitive medical instruments from the Civil War.	Build a model of a Civil War site.
Research primary documents.	Look at photographs.	Participate in a debate.	Compare a prominent African American hero to self.	Study demographics from then and now.	Listen to blues.	Look at maps of Africa and the United States.	Stage a historical reenactment.
Read the biography of Lincoln (or another historical figure).	Create family trees.	Interview an African American businessperson.	Keep a journal from the viewpoint of a soldier, slave, or family member.	Compile statistics on health, schools, jobs, pay scales, crime, contributions, and military contributions during Civil War.	Listen to gospel.	Collect and categorize photos of African American migration.	Take a field trip to a Civil War cemetery.
Read *Cold Mountain*.	Create a collage of African American history.	Blog about African American issues.	Find a personal connection to the topic.	Study the economic status and improvements of African Americans.	Listen to rap.	Study African tribes.	Visit an African American history museum.
Read a book about Gettysburg.	Create a Martin Luther King Jr. memorial.	Participate in a peer dialogue on injustices.	Write poetry.	Study populations and demographics.	Listen to African music.	Study African regions.	Make drama costumes.
Read the Harriet Tubman story.	Study maps and graphic displays.	Role-play with a partner.	Write a letter to Oprah.	Study graphs, charts, and statistical implications.	Give a performance or do a role-play about slavery.	Study the Underground Railroad and the path to freedom.	Perform the musical *The Color Purple*.
Write about a current issue as an op-ed piece.	Tell the Obama story.	Role-play problem scenarios in small groups.	Look at profiles of courage.	Collect or draw currency of the Civil War era.	Study composers of the period.	Visit a Civil War cemetery.	Build cartoon model of characters of the period.

Figure 9.4: High school curriculum unit on African American history.

Following is an Action Option for PLC teams to try in regard to planning with differentiation in mind. The Gallery Walk is used to observe various curriculum planning grids from team members. We've also included two reproducibles. The "Multimodal Curriculum Unit Template" (page 159) is a primary tool for teams to talk about upcoming units of study and how to differentiate activity options and assessment options. This template keeps the team on the same page, so to speak, as members use similar elements in their initial planning tools. The "Multimodal Grid of Activities" (pages 160–161) is a cheat sheet of sorts that includes actions, word associations, and activities for each intelligence to help teams jump-start the brainstorming process. (Visit **go.solution-tree.com/instruction** to download all reproducibles in this book.)

Action Option 1: The Gallery Walk

Teachers, as teams of two or three who have worked together or as individuals, display their grids on the training room walls for the entire PLC team to review and for other teams to preview or view. Those viewing the grids move around the room as if walking through an art gallery. Instead of passively observing, however, they are encouraged to post comments and suggestions on the work via sticky notes. The results are visible evidence of collaboration, and the comments become documentation of the group's collective wisdom.

As curriculum units are in the process of being designed, they can also be displayed in the staff room so that members of other teams, department heads, and the administration can view them. There are many benefits to this strategy. First, by displaying the artifacts as a work in progress, colleagues can learn as much about the process of designing a unit as they can about the final product. Second, colleagues are invited to post encouraging comments on the artifacts. The feedback is visible to the entire school and has a dynamic, multiplying effect. Third, sharing the collegial thinking process reinforces and supports the idea of schools as learning communities. The positive impact is contagious and lasting.

Multimodal Curriculum Unit Template

Grade:

Subject:

Topic(s):

Standard(s):

Big Ideas:

Tagline:

Essential Question:

Verbal	Visual	Interpersonal	Intrapersonal	Mathematical	Musical	Naturalist	Bodily

Multimodal Grid of Activities

Verbal	Visual	Interpersonal	Intrapersonal	Mathematical	Musical	Naturalist	Bodily
Discussion	Diagram	Partners	Journals	Calculate	Muzak	Classify	Hands-on
Debrief	Draw	Pairs	Self-monitoring	Compute	Beat	Sort	Kinesthetic
Speaking	Sketches	Communication	Metacognition	Problem solve	Melody	Plants	Tactile
Articulate	Graphic organizers	Dialogue	Self-awareness	Deduction	Tunes	Feed animals	Touch
Debate	Doodle	Articulation	Self-appraisal	Induction	Songs	Garden	Taste
Reading	Photographs	Talking	Dialogues	Sequence	Rhythms	Explore	Smell
Expressing	Represent	Arguing	Reflecting	Prioritize	Raps	Discover	Senses
Paraphrase	Drawings	Agreeing	Musings	Hierarchies	Blues	Astronomy	Construct
Narratives	Painting	Disagreeing	Thinking	Puzzles	Jazz	Relationships	Feel
Novels	Images	Team building	Observing	Riddles	Rock and roll	Charting	Cut
Storytelling	Cartoons	Leadership	Analyzing	Outlines	Score	Dissecting	Paste
Tell and retell	Comics	Teaming	Self-control	Cause and effect	Harmony	Watching	Arrange
Writing	Illustrations	Group work	Self-esteem	Theories	Listening	Identifying	Organize
Crosswords	Charts	Teamwork	Introspection	Theorems	Appreciating	Collecting	Dance
Listening	Graphs	Consensus	Inner voice	Equations	Jingles	Investigating	Move
Riddles	Tables	Games	Intuition	Formulas	Composing	Hiking	Act

Verbal	Visual	Interpersonal	Intrapersonal	Mathematical	Musical	Naturalist	Bodily
Joke	Maps	Relays	Hunches	Symbols	Conducting	Growing	Sculpt
Summary	Murals	Roles	Gut feelings	Codes	Drumming	Climbing	Walk
Magazines	Collages	Responsibilities	Instinct	Syllogisms	Whistling	Uncovering	Dramatize
Journals	Visualize	Socializing	Goals	Probabilities	Humming	Forecasting	Signal
Bibliography	Signs	Meeting	Learning logs	Statistics	Performing	Catching	Gesture
Biography	Storyboard	Greeting	Diaries	Evaluate	Singing	Wading	Pantomime
Research	View	Sharing	Affirmations	Estimate	Lyrics	Fishing	Role-play
Blogs	Pictures	Interactions	Study	Hypothesis	Playing	Floating	Stretch
Newspapers	Internet	Chat rooms	Empathy	Systematize	Improve	Capture	Mimic
Interviews	Movies	Networking	Dreams	Configure	Scat singing	Surviving	Gesture
Speeches	Faces	Pillow talk	Sixth sense	Appraisal	Synchronization	Orienteering	Dance

CHAPTER **10**

NEXT STEPS

PLC TAKE AWAY

Learning How Teachers Decide on the Next Student-Success Priority

The journey of PLC teams who have decided to focus on differentiation as a student-centered instructional goal—if given enough time and commitment—will eventually reach the final phase of Fullan and Stiegelbauer's (1991) model of change, discussed in depth in chapter 2: institutionalization.

At this stage, data-driven differentiated instruction becomes an integral part of all the work teachers in PLCs do with instruction, curriculum, and assessment. Institutionalization means that data and differentiation are part of the landscape of teachers' classrooms and PLC team meetings. It means that the sharing, the learning, and the differentiation theory and practices are explicitly passed along and integrated into the orientation of every new member of the PLC teams. Institutionalizing differentiated instruction ensures it is part of the way things are done with all PLC teams in the learning community and is part and parcel of the culture and spirit that PLCs embrace.

As differentiation is incorporated into the culture of the PLCs and the school, the teams may need to revisit their goals. They may talk about refreshing the goal in regard to certain aspects that need more attention, or they may decide to cycle on to another pressing concern. After all, this is about a community where the learning is ongoing.

Setting New Agendas

Acting on the past, PLCs often are faced with setting new agendas. Attaching a timeline to these agendas serves the continuous, unending work of professional learning communities. Following are two sample timelines for implementing differentiation. The first is for one term (fig. 10.1). This often suits the planning of middle and high school PLC teams. The second (fig. 10.2) is for the entire year, which may be more appropriate for elementary-level team planning.

The one-term timeline condenses the planning to five months. In this way, it is perceived as an achievable goal for teams that work on a semester schedule. To achieve a goal in this shorter time frame, however, the schedule is front-loaded for early preparation in August and September. Teams within PLCs can use the example as a guide to tailor their own timelines. (See pages 169–170 for reproducibles of these agendas. Visit **go.solution-tree.com/instruction** to download all reproducibles in this book.)

Goal: Differentiated instruction	
August– September	Summer reading: select book about differentiated instruction. Discuss book. Examine available student data; identify student talent and needs. List known strategies for developing or struggling learners, advanced or gifted learners, English learners, and learners with special needs. Commit to differentiation as a concept and as a practice.
October	Focus on changing something for whole-class options: explicit practice and reflective dialogue about changing content, process, and products.
November	Focus on lesson design for whole-class differentiation: explicit practice and reflective dialogue about revising old lessons and developing new lessons that incorporate differentiation to reach and teach all students.
December	Focus on differentiated curriculum unit for whole-class options: explicit practice in designing one differentiated curriculum unit using the multimodal activity grid as part of the team planning.
January	Focus on implementation of differentiated instruction for data-driven flexible skill groups: explicit practice in forming flexible skill groups as needed by examining data, planning instructional interventions, and monitoring progress with formative assessments and team reflection on differentiation goal—what's working, what's not, what's next (writing common assessments, studying data, creating interventions, and so on).

Figure 10.1: Semester-length timeline for differentiating instruction.

Next, we'll look at a school-year goal schedule. It is a natural and manageable time-line for elementary schools where teacher teams have the same students all year for all subjects. However, this timeline can be adjusted as teams decide what works best for them.

Goal: Differentiated instruction	
August–September	Summer reading: select book about differentiated instruction. Discuss book. Examine available student data; identify student talent and needs Commit to differentiation as a concept and as a practice.
October	Focus on learner archetypes: explicit practice and reflective dialogue in identifying known strategies for developing or struggling learners, advanced or gifted learners, English learners, and learners with special needs.
November	Focus on changing something for whole-class options: explicit practice and reflective dialogue about changing the content of the lesson through complexity, resources, and environment.
December	Focus on process of lesson: explicit practice and reflective dialogue about direct-instruction, cooperative-learning inquiry models.
January	Focus on product of lesson: explicit practice and reflective dialogue about changing the products through entry points, exit points, and accountability.
February	Focus on lesson design for whole-class differentiation: explicit practice and reflective dialogue in revising old lessons and developing new lessons that incorporate differentiation to reach and teach all students.
March	Focus on reflective practice of differentiation: explicit practice in color coding evidence of differentiation in lessons, units, assessments, and debriefing dialogues within the PLC teams.
April	Focus on differentiated curriculum unit for whole-class options: explicit practice in designing one differentiated curriculum unit using the multi-modal activity grid as part of the team planning within the PLC.
May	Focus on implementation of differentiated instruction for data-driven flexible skill groups: explicit practice in forming flexible skill groups as needed by examining data, planning instructional interventions, and monitoring progress with formative assessments. Reflect on differentiation goal.
June	Focus on reflective dialogue about the differentiation goal: What's working? What's not? Future planning: What next? Why? (writing common assessments, reviewing data, creating interventions, and so on)

Figure 10.2: School-year-length timeline for differentiating instruction.

Again, the timelines are simply examples of how PLC teams might plan for and schedule a team initiative. It just matters that there is some kind of long-term plan to provide needed parameters for the work of the PLC teams. The sample schedules are presented to provide a visual of what the long-term plan might look like as PLCs develop their own planning schemes.

Structured discussions about what's working and what's not, what next steps might be, what emergent ideas are pending, and what specific target goals make sense are the norm of highly functioning teams and flourishing PLCs. When one goal seems in good standing, the teams take time to reflect and redefine their purpose, intentions, and needs. This period can be tumultuous as the teams maintain and sustain the differentiation focus while simultaneously settling on the next challenge and transitioning, gingerly, to that focus.

To that end, we've included two Action Options that PLCs can choose to structure the transition toward subsequent target goals. In the meantime, teachers in PLCs should continue to shepherd differentiated instruction in all their instructional endeavors.

In closing, it is now time to look back on the journey just completed, begin the next journey to come for the team, or—depending on how the book has been used thus far—find another chapter of interest to pursue. In any case, keep in mind that the journey is as important as the destination. The progression of the learning organization, propelled by collaborative conversations, supports the ongoing work of the professional. The destination is the student success that results from the culture of learning and the continuous improvement in instruction through the differentiation process. Choose that next PLC challenge carefully, and get it going right away.

Action Options

> **PLC TAKE AWAY**
>
> Learning How Teachers Decide on the Next Student-Success Priority

PLC teams often must reinvent themselves every school year (and sometimes during the school year) to accommodate changes in staff and the arrival of new students. Just as veteran teachers approach the first days of school in a more comfortable way, since they are prepared for the unexpected, so too do established, ongoing teams within PLCs. They understand and anticipate the possibilities and the challenges as they venture forth with a new year, a new team, new kids, and new goals.

Each time teams of teachers working with a PLC experience major changes, they are wise to revisit their basic mission and the fundamental tenets of the leaders of the PLC movement. A PLC is made up of educators committed to working collaboratively in ongoing processes of collective inquiry and action research to achieve better results for the students they serve. Professional learning communities operate under the assumption that the key to improved learning for students is continuous job-embedded learning for educators. (DuFour et al., 2006, p. 217)

The final Action Options include a reflective exercise—Bridging Snapshots—designed to reflect on the work done and the connections, insights, and lessons learned, and Action Plan and Timeline, a planning exercise with timelines attached. Visit www .allthingsplc.info/tools/print.php#21 for PowerPoint presentations on curriculum and assessment.

Action Option 1: Bridging Snapshots

This strategy works as a review of previous learning, but can also be used as a resource for planning. Working in pairs, PLC team members divide a poster-sized sheet into twelve boxes or "snapshot" frames. Within the twelve boxes, the pairs randomly write down any moment, decision, instance, or event that they remember from the process of differentiating goals. The items might be minor adjustments or major changes of direction. For example, they may write "first differentiated lesson," "color-coded differentiation," "unit—big idea and tagline," or "culminating project." It doesn't matter as long as the pairs have twelve ideas represented. This strategy is designed to activate the memory.

Once they have noted all these memories, the pairs draw lines to connect or bridge the snapshots, while talking and sharing ideas about what actually occurred and how it evolved. Note that these lines need not be chronological necessarily, but rather spontaneous, random connections. These snapshots—some small accomplishments, some larger—become a tangible historical record. The result is a rich dialogue of reflection and accomplishment, as the members fill in blanks in their memory to clarify all they have done on their journey as a dedicated community of learners.

This record sets the stage for future planning as the members of the PLCs look over what they have done, where they have been, and what changes in direction and new courses of action they have experienced. This teacher-tested, time-proven reflection activity yields much insight and introspection.

Action Option 2: Action Plan and Timeline

Following are reproducibles of a semester-length agenda and a school-year-length agenda to help teams begin planning the next steps. Teams should make decisions about an appropriate timeline based on what grade levels they teach and what makes the most sense for their particular situations. These decisions should occur in team meetings either at the end of each school year or term or at the beginning of the next.

Usually, teams revisit and revise the strategic planning guide along the way. Some teams may find it more helpful than others. It behooves teams, however, to at least begin with this kind of macrodiscussion. The samples provided can be used as is, or teams can use them as templates for developing their own strategic schedules.

Semester-Length Timeline for Differentiating Instruction

Goal: Differentiated instruction	
August–September	
October	
November	
December	
January	

School-Year-Length Timeline for Differentiating Instruction

Goal: Differentiated instruction	
August–September	
October	
November	
December	
January	
February	
March	
April	
May	
June	

REFERENCES AND RESOURCES

Allard, H. (1977). *Miss Nelson is missing!* Boston: Houghton Mifflin.

Armstrong, T. (1999). *7 kinds of smart: Identifying and developing your multiple intelligences.* New York: Plume.

Atchison, D. (Writer/Director). (2006). *Akeelah and the bee* [Motion picture]. United States: Out of the Blue Entertainment.

Backer, L., Deck, M., & McCallum, D. (1995). *The presenter's survival kit, it's a jungle out there!* St. Louis, MO: Mosby.

Barrows, H. S., & Tamblyn, R. M. (1980). *Problem-based learning: An approach to medical education.* New York: Springer.

Belgrade, S., Burke, K., & Fogarty, R. (2008). *The portfolio connection: Student work linked to standards.* Thousand Oaks, CA: Corwin Press.

Bellanca, J. (2009). *Designing professional development for change: A guide for improving classroom instruction* (2nd ed.). Thousand Oaks, CA: Corwin Press.

Bellanca, J. (2010). *Enriched learning projects: A practical pathway to 21st century skills.* Bloomington, IN: Solution Tree Press.

Bellanca, J., & Fogarty, R. (2003). *Blueprints for thinking in the cooperative classroom* (3rd ed.). Glenview, IL: Pearson/Skylight.

Berman, S. (1999). *Service learning for the multiple intelligences classroom.* Arlington Heights, IL: Skylight.

Bishop, C. H., & Wiese, K. (1996). *The five Chinese brothers.* New York: Penguin Putnam Books for Young Readers.

Bloom, B. S. (Ed.). (1956). *Taxonomy of educational objectives, handbook 1: Cognitive domain.* New York: David McKay.

Bogdanovich, P. (Director), & Hamilton Phelan, A. (Writer). (1985). *Mask* [Motion picture]. United States: Universal Pictures.

Burke, K. (2009). *How to assess authentic learning* (5th ed.). Thousand Oaks, CA: Corwin Press.

Caine, R. N., Caine, G., McClintic, C., & Klimek, K. J. (2009). *12 brain/mind learning principles in action: Developing executive functions of the human brain* (2nd ed.). Thousand Oaks, CA: Corwin Press.

Chapman, C., & King, R. (2003). *Differentiated instructional strategies for reading in the content areas.* Thousand Oaks, CA: Corwin Press.

Chenoweth, K. (2007). *It's being done: Academic success in unexpected schools.* Cambridge, MA: Harvard Education Press.

Chenoweth, K. (2009). It can be done, it's being done, and here's how. *Phi Delta Kappan, 91*(1), 39–43.

Clare, J. D. (2004). Differentiation. *Greenfield School and Community Arts College.* Accessed at www.greenfield.durham.sch.uk/differentiation.htm on June 16, 2010.

Collier, M. (2008). Amusing out-dated laws. *Associated Content.* Accessed at www.associatedcontent.com/article/1228232/amusing_outdated_laws_html?cat=17 on July 22, 2010.

Costa, A. (2008). *School as a home for the mind: Creating mindful curriculum, instruction, and dialogue* (2nd ed.). Thousand Oaks, CA: Corwin Press.

Costa, A., & Kallick, B. (2009). *Habits of mind across the curriculum: Practical and creative strategies for teachers.* Alexandria, VA: Association for Supervision and Curriculum Development.

Creech, S. (2001). *A fine, fine school.* New York: Joanna Cotler Books/HarperCollins.

Csikszentmihalyi, M. (1990). *Flow: The psychology of optimal experience.* New York: Harper and Row.

Darling-Hammond, L. (2009). *Developing learning-centered schools for students and teachers.* Thousand Oaks, CA: SAGE.

Deming, W. E. (2000). *Out of the crisis.* Cambridge, MA: MIT Press.

Dewey, J. (1916). *Democracy and education: An introduction to the philosophy of education.* New York: Macmillan.

Diamond, M., & Hopson, J. (1998). *Magic trees of the mind: How to nurture your child's intelligence, creativity, and healthy emotions from birth through adolescence.* New York: Dutton.

DuFour, R., DuFour, R., & Eaker, R. (2008). *Revisiting professional learning communities at work: New insights for improving schools.* Bloomington, IN: Solution Tree Press.

DuFour, R., DuFour, R., Eaker, R., & Karhanek, G. (2004). *Whatever it takes: How professional learning communities respond when kids don't learn.* Bloomington, IN: Solution Tree Press.

DuFour, R., DuFour, R., Eaker, R., & Karhanek, G. (2010). *Raising the bar and closing the gap: Whatever it takes.* Bloomington, IN: Solution Tree Press.

DuFour, R., DuFour, R., Eaker, R., & Many, T. (2006). *Learning by doing: A handbook for professional learning communities at work.* Bloomington, IN: Solution Tree Press.

DuFour, R., & Eaker, R. (1998). *Professional learning communities at work: Best practices for enhancing student achievement.* Bloomington, IN: Solution Tree Press.

Dunn, R., & Dunn, K. (1998). *The Dunn and Dunn learning style model of instruction.* Unpublished research paper, University of California, Los Angeles.

Feuerstein, R., Klein, P., & Tannenbaum, A. (1999). *Mediated learning experience (MLE): Theoretical, psychosocial and learning implications.* Tel Aviv, Israel: Freund.

Finchler, J. (2000). *Testing Miss Malarkey.* New York: Walker and Company.

Fogarty, R. (1997). *Problem-based learning and other curriculum models for the multiple intelligences classroom.* Arlington Heights, IL: IRI/Skylight.

Fogarty, R. (1999). *Balanced assessment.* Thousand Oaks, CA: Corwin Press.

Fogarty, R. (2001a). *The roots of change. Journal of Staff Development, 22*(3), 34–36.

Fogarty, R. (2001b). *Teachers make the difference: A framework for quality.* Chicago: Robin Fogarty and Associates.

Fogarty, R. (2009). *Brain-compatible classrooms* (3rd ed.). Thousand Oaks, CA: Corwin Press.

Fogarty, R., & Kerns, G. (2009). *Informative assessment: When it's not about a grade.* Thousand Oaks, CA: Corwin Press.

Fogarty, R., & Pete, B. (2004a). *The adult learner: Some things we know.* Thousand Oaks, CA: Corwin Press.

Fogarty, R., & Pete, B. (2004b). *A look at transfer: Seven strategies that work.* Thousand Oaks, CA: Corwin Press.

Fogarty, R., & Pete, B. (2007a). *From staff room to classroom: A guide for planning and coaching professional development.* Thousand Oaks, CA: Corwin Press.

Fogarty, R., & Pete, B. (2007b). *How to differentiate learning: Curriculum, instruction, and assessment.* Thousand Oaks, CA: Corwin Press.

Fogarty, R., & Pete, B. (2009). *How to integrate the curricula* (3rd ed.). Thousand Oaks, CA: Corwin Press.

Fogarty, R., & Stoehr, J. (2008). *Integrating curricula with multiple intelligences: Teams, themes, and threads* (2nd ed.). Thousand Oaks, CA: Corwin Press.

Forward, T. (2004). *The first day of school.* London: Corgi.

Fox, M. (1985). *Wilfrid Gordon McDonald Partridge.* Brooklyn, NY: Kane/Miller.

Fullan, M., Hill, P., & Crévola, C. (2006). *Breakthrough.* Thousand Oaks, CA: Corwin Press.

Fullan, M., & Stiegelbauer, S. (1991). *The new meaning of educational change.* New York: Teachers College Press.

Gardner, H. (1983). *Frames of mind: The theory of multiple intelligences.* New York: Basic Books.

Gardner, H. (1999). *Intelligence reframed: Multiple intelligences for the 21st century.* New York: Basic Books.

Gladwell, M. (2002). *The tipping point: How little things can make a big difference.* Boston: Back Bay Books.

Graham, P., & Ferriter, W. (2008). One step at a time: Many professional learning teams pass through these 7 stages. *Journal of Staff Development, 29*(3), 38–42.

Grant, J., & Forsten, C. (1999). *If you're riding a horse and it dies, get off.* Peterborough, NH: Crystal Springs Books.

Gregorc, A. (1982). *An adult's guide to style.* Chicago: Gregorc Associates.

Gregory, G. H., & Chapman, C. (2007). *Differentiated instructional strategies: One size doesn't fit all* (2nd ed.). Thousand Oaks, CA: Corwin Press.

Gregory, G. H., & Kuzmich, L. (2004). *Data driven differentiation in the standards-based classroom.* Thousand Oaks, CA: Corwin Press.

Guskey, T. R. (2000). *Evaluating professional development.* Thousand Oaks, CA: Corwin Press.

Harris, T. A. (2004). *I'm ok, you're ok.* New York: HarperCollins.

Haycock, K. (2009). Students can't wait for strong teachers. *When the going gets tough: Smart choices, bold action.* Paper presented at the 2009 Education Trust National Conference, Arlington, VA. Accessed at www2.edtrust .org/EdTrust/Conferences+and+Meetings on June 15, 2010.

Herek, S. (Director), & Duncan, P. S. (Writer). (1995). *Mr. Holland's opus* [Motion picture]. United States: Hollywood Pictures.

Holmes, O. W. (1924). *The poet at the breakfast table.* New York: E. P. Dutton and Company.

Hord, S., & Sommers, W. (2009). *Leading professional learning communities: Voices from research and practice.* Thousand Oaks, CA: Corwin Press.

Hunter, M. (1995). *Teach for transfer.* Thousand Oaks, CA: Corwin Press.

Hyerle, D. (2009). *Visual tools for transforming information into knowledge* (2nd ed.). Thousand Oaks, CA: Corwin Press.

Individuals With Disabilities Education Act, 20 U.S.C. § 1400. (1990).

Jacobs, H. H. (Ed.). (1989). *Interdisciplinary curriculum: Design and implementation.* Alexandria, VA: Association for Supervision and Curriculum Development.

Jensen, E. (2008). *Brain-based learning: The new paradigm of teaching* (2nd ed.). Thousand Oaks, CA: Corwin Press.

Jímenez, F. (1998). *La mariposa.* Boston: Houghton Mifflin.

Johnson, D. W., & Johnson R. T. (1998). *Cooperative learning and social interdependence theory.* Accessed at www.co-operation.org/pages/SIT.html on July 22, 2010.

Johnson, D. W., Johnson, R. T., & Holubec, E. J. (1986). *Circles of learning: Cooperation in the classroom.* Edina, MN: Interaction Book Company.

Jones, R. (1996). *The acorn people.* New York: Bantam Doubleday.

Joyce, B., & Showers, B. (2002). *Student achievement through staff development* (3rd ed.). Alexandria, VA: Association of Supervision and Curriculum Development.

Kagan, S. (1989). The structural approach to cooperative learning. *Educational Leadership, 47*(4), 12–15.

Kagan, S. (1994). *Cooperative learning.* San Clemente, CA: Kagan.

Killion, J. (1999). Skill shop: Knowing when, and how much, to intervene. *Journal of Staff Development, 20*(1), 59–60.

Knowles, M. S. (1973). *The adult learner: A neglected species.* Houston, TX: Gulf.

Knowles, M. S., Holton, E. F., III, & Swanson, R. A. (1998). *The adult learner: The definitive classic in adult education and human resource development* (5th ed.). Houston, TX: Gulf.

Kotter, J. P. (1996). *Leading change.* Boston: Harvard Business School Press.

Krause, R. (1971). *Leo the late bloomer.* New York: Windmill Books.

LaGravenese, R. (Writer/Director). (2007). *Freedom writers* [Motion picture]. United States: Paramount Pictures.

Lieberman, A. (Ed.). (1988). *Building a professional culture in schools.* New York: Teachers College Press.

Lieberman, A., & Miller, L. (2000). Teaching and teacher development: A new synthesis for a new century. In R. S. Brandt, *Education in a new era* (pp. 47–66).

Alexandria, VA: Association for Supervision and Curriculum Development. Accessed at www.ascd.org/publications/books/100000/chapters/Teaching -and-Teacher-Development@-A-New-Synthesis-for-a-New-Century.aspx on July 26, 2010.

Lindsay, J. (2000). *Jane Goodall: Forty years at Gombe.* New York: Stewart, Tabori and Chang.

Lortie, D. (1975). *Schoolteacher: A sociological study.* Chicago: University of Chicago Press.

Marcus, S. A. (2007). *The hungry brain: The nutrition/cognition connection.* Thousand Oaks, CA: Corwin Press.

Marzano, R., Pickering, D., & McTighe, J. (1993). *Assessing student outcomes: Performance assessment using the Dimensions of Learning model.* Alexandria, VA: Association for Supervision and Curriculum Development.

Marzano, R., Pickering, D., & Pollock, J. (2001). *Classroom instruction that works: Researched-based strategies for increasing student achievement.* Alexandria, VA: Association for Supervision and Curriculum Development.

Mora, P. (2003). *The rainbow tulip.* New York: Puffin Books.

Myers, I. B. (1962). *Introduction to type: A guide to understanding your results on the Myers-Briggs Type Indicator.* Palo Alto, CA: Consulting Psychologists Press.

National Council of Gifted Education. (2008). Is there a definition of "gifted"? *Frequently asked questions.* Accessed at www.nagc.org/index2.aspx?id=548 on July 22, 2010.

Parnes, S. (1975). *Aha insights into creative behavior.* Buffalo, NY: D. O. K.

Perkins, D., & Salomon, G. (2001). Teaching for transfer. In A. L. Costa (Ed.), *Developing minds: A resource book for teaching thinking* (3rd ed.). Alexandria, VA: Association for Supervision and Curriculum Development.

Pete, B., & Duncan, C. (2004). *Data! Dialogue! Decisions! The data difference.* Thousand Oaks, CA: Corwin Press.

Pete, B., & Fogarty, R. (2003). *Nine best practices that make the difference.* Thousand Oaks, CA: Corwin Press.

Pete, B., & Fogarty, R. (2005). *Close the achievement gap: Simple strategies that work.* Thousand Oaks, CA: Corwin Press.

Pete, B., & Fogarty, R. (2007). *Twelve brain principles that make the difference.* Thousand Oaks, CA: Corwin Press.

Pete, B., & Fogarty, R. (2010). *From staff room to classroom II: The one-minute professional development planner.* Thousand Oaks, CA: Corwin Press.

Piaget, J., & Inhelder, B. (2000). *The psychology of the child.* New York: Basic Books.

Picoult, J. (2004). *My sister's keeper.* New York: Atria Books.

Polacco, P. (1998). *Thank you, Mr. Falker.* New York: Philomel Books.

Reeves, D. (2002). *Making standards work: How to implement standards-based assessments in the classroom, school, and district* (3rd ed.). Denver, CO: Advanced Learning Press.

Reynolds, P. H. (2003). *The dot.* Cambridge, MA: Candlewick Press.

Richardson, J. (2009). Quality education is our moon shot: An interview with Secretary of Education Arne Duncan. *Phi Delta Kappan, 91*(1), 24–29.

Sarasan, S. (1982). *The culture of school and the problem of change* (2nd ed.). Boston: Allyn & Bacon.

Schmoker, M. (1996). *Results: The key to continuous school improvement.* Alexandria, VA: Association of Supervision and Curriculum Development.

Schmuck, R. (1997). *Practical action research for change.* Arlington Heights, IL: IRI/Skylight.

Schmuck, R., & Schmuck, P. (1997). *Group processes in the classroom* (7th ed.). Madison, WI: Brown and Benchmark.

Shriver, M. (2001). *What's wrong with Timmy?* Boston: Little, Brown and Company.

Sollman, C. (1994). *Through the cracks.* Worcester, MA: Davis.

Sousa, D. (1995). *How the brain learns.* Reston, VA: National Association of Secondary School Principals.

Sparks, D., & Hirsh, S. (1997). *A new vision for staff development.* Alexandria, VA: Association for Supervision and Curriculum Development.

Sparks, D., & Loucks-Horsley, S. (1989). Five models of staff development. *Journal of Staff Development, 10*(4). Accessed at www.nsdc.org/news/jsd/sparks104.cfm on July 26, 2010.

Sternberg, R. (1988). *Beyond IQ: A triarchic theory of human intelligence.* New York: Cambridge University Press.

Stiggins, R. (2005). From formative assessment to assessment FOR learning: A path to success in standards-based schools. *Phi Delta Kappan, 87*(4), 324–328.

Stronge, J. (2002). *Qualities of effective teachers.* Alexandria, VA: Association for Supervision and Curriculum Development.

Swift, J. (1996). *A modest proposal and other satirical works.* New York: Dover.

Sylwester, R. (1995). *A celebration of neurons: An educator's guide to the human brain.* Alexandria, VA: Association for Supervision and Curriculum Development.

Tate, M. (2004). *Lessons learned: 20 instructional strategies that engage the adult mind.* Thousand Oaks, CA: Corwin Press.

Tomlinson, C. A. (1999a). *The differentiated classroom: Responding to the needs of all learners*. Alexandria, VA: Association for Supervision and Curriculum Development.

Tomlinson, C. A. (1999b). Mapping a route toward differentiated curriculum. *Educational Leadership, 57*(1), 12–16.

Tomlinson, C. A. (2000). Reconcilable differences? Standards-based teaching and differentiation. *Educational Leadership, 58*(1), 6–11.

Tomlinson, C. A. (2001). *How to differentiate in mixed-ability classrooms* (2nd ed.). Alexandria, VA: Association for Supervision and Curriculum Development.

Tomlinson, C. A. (2003). Deciding to teach them all. *Educational Leadership, 61*(2), 6–11.

Tomlinson, C. A., & Callahan, C. M. (1992). Contributions of gifted education to general education in a time of change. *Gifted Child Quarterly, 36*(4), 183–189.

Tomlinson, C. A., & Cunningham Eidson, C. (2003). *Differentiation in practice: A resource guide for differentiating curriculum grades K–5*. Alexandria, VA: Association for Supervision and Curriculum Development

Van Wie, N. A. (1999). *Travels with Max: How a bill becomes a law*. Venice, FL: Max's.

Vygotsky, L. S. (1978). *Mind in society: The development of higher psychological processes* (14th ed.). Cambridge, MA: Harvard University Press.

Wang, N., & Taraban, R. (1997). *Do learning strategies affect adults' transfer of learning?* (ERIC Document Reproduction Service No. ED413419)

Wiggins, G., & McTighe, J. (2005). *Understanding by design* (2nd ed.). Alexandria, VA: Association for Supervision and Curriculum Development.

Williams, R. B. (1996a). Four dimensions of the school change facilitator. *Journal of Staff Development, 17*(1), 48–50.

Williams, R. B. (1996b). *More than 50 ways to build team consensus* [Training package]. Arlington Heights, IL: Skylight.

Williams, R. B. (2008). *12 roles of facilitators for school change* (2nd ed.). Thousand Oaks, CA: Corwin Press.

Wong, H. K., & Wong, R. T. (1998). *The first days of school: How to be an effective teacher* (2nd ed.). Mountainview, CA: Harry K. Wong.

Zemke, R., & Zemke, S. (1981). 30 things we know for sure about adult learning. *Training, 4*(8), 45–52.

INDEX

Learning by Doing: A Handbook for Professional Learning Communities at Work™ (Second Edition)
Richard DuFour, Rebecca DuFour, Robert Eaker, and Thomas Many
The second edition of this pivotal action guide includes seven major additions that equip educators with essential tools for confronting challenges. **BKF416**

Raising the Bar and Closing the Gap: Whatever It Takes
Richard DuFour, Rebecca DuFour, Robert Eaker, and Gayle Karhanek
This sequel to the best-selling *Whatever It Takes: How Professional Learning Communities Respond When Kids Don't Learn* expands on original ideas and presses further with new insights. **BKF378**

Differentiation and the Brain: How Neuroscience Supports the Learner-Friendly Classroom
David A. Sousa and Carol Ann Tomlinson
Examine the basic principles of differentiation in light of educational neuroscience research that will help you make the most effective curricular, instructional, and assessment choices. **BKF353**

21st Century Skills: Rethinking How Students Learn
Edited by James Bellanca and Ron Brandt
Education luminaries reveal why 21st century skills are necessary, which skills are most important, and how to help schools include them in curriculum and instruction. **BKF389**

Solution Tree | Press *a division of*
Solution Tree

Visit solution-tree.com or call 800.733.6786 to order.